ANTHROPOLOGY IN NORWAY

Royal Anthropological Institute

The RAI Country Series

Series Editor: David Shankland

A series of publications celebrating the traditions of anthropology in different countries. Not assuming any essential national identity, but rather – noting the pragmatic reality that anthropology may follow markedly different trajectories in different places – exploring how the discipline has taken shape, being both influenced by its wider social, cultural and intellectual setting and helping to create it.

Volume 1   *Anthropology at the Crossroads: The View from France*
            edited by Sophie Chevalier

Volume 2   *Twilight Zone Anthropology: Voices from Poland*
            edited by Michał Buchowski

Volume 3   *Anthropology in Norway: Directions, Locations, Relations*
            edited by Synnøve K.N. Bendixsen and Edvard Hviding

Volume 4   *Anthropology in Motion: Encounters with Current Trajectories
            of Scholarship from Austria*
            edited by Andre Gingrich

Volume 5   *Social Anthropologies of the Welsh: Past and Present*
            edited by W. John Morgan and Fiona Bowie

Anthropology in Norway

Directions, Locations, Relations

EDITED BY SYNNØVE K.N. BENDIXSEN

AND EDVARD HVIDING

The RAI Country Series, Volume Three

SK Publishing

Sean Kingston Publishing

www.seankingston.co.uk

Canon Pyon

First published in 2021 by
Sean Kingston Publishing
www.seankingston.co.uk
Canon Pyon

British Library Cataloguing in Publication Data
A catalogue record for this book is available from the British Library.
The moral rights of the editor and authors have been asserted.

Paperback ISBN 978-1-912385-30-0

Ebook DOI 10.26581/B.BEND01

FOREWORD

As the editors of this splendid volume explain in their introduction, this work stems from the series of days that we have held at the RAI to celebrate the way anthropology has taken shape in different countries around the world. In the UK, we have long admired anthropology in Norway, and it was therefore natural that we should seek to learn more. We were therefore delighted to welcome colleagues to a Norwegian Anthropology Day, which took place in the British Academy, where we enjoyed an extraordinarily fruitful encounter. Indeed, the scintillating discussion and different areas that we were able to explore remain long in the memory. I should like to thank Edvard Hviding, and all our colleagues from Norway, for their wonderful contribution, from which we gained a great deal, both in the social interactions and in the formal presentations.

In discussing this series, I am sometimes asked as to the wisdom of holding national days of anthropology, as this has connotations that a global discipline such as ours would not usually, at least without many qualifications, embrace. I am pleased, then to clarify that therefore we have carefully chosen the word 'country' rather than 'national' for this reason. We would not wish, for a moment, to suggest that intellectual traditions take shape in isolation, nor indeed that anthropology could be as it is, and should be, if it gets too close to any 'national' project. Indeed, the reverse: it is almost a definition of modern social anthropology that it has emerged as an inherently transnational project, and has almost always been uncertain as to its relations with national authorities.

This said, it is also clearly the case that the way that anthropology has taken root in different countries differs, and we can learn much about the history of our discipline, as well as its contemporary relevance, by exploring the way that it has flourished, or in some case encountered difficulties. The relationship between social anthropology and museums is one obvious such area, another is the dynamic between anthropology at home, and overseas; yet another is the relationship between ethnography and social anthropology, or indeed the breadth of the discipline. All these areas are mentioned and explored in the rich papers that are found here.

When we look across the North Sea, we are struck at the enormous contribution to public life that anthropology in Norway has made. It would not be quite right to say that we are envious of such success, for we applaud and admire it. Nevertheless, we are conscious that we have a great deal to learn in Britain as to how we may best go about this, and the example of our colleagues in Norway offers profound food for thought.

All of us working at the RAI, along with the Fellows and Council of the Institute, join me in offering our thanks and best wishes for the future of anthropology in Norway, and we look forward greatly to our future encounters.

David Shankland
Director, Royal Anthropological Institute

Acknowledgements

The Norwegian Anthropology Day took place on Friday 30 October 2015 – and thus the present volume has been long in the making, which is the result of a series of circumstances, some of which have been beyond our control and some of which relate to conflicting obligations, changing job situations and other factors. We hope the qualities of the book can in the end justify some of the waiting.

We would like first of all to express our gratitude and sincere thanks to the Royal Anthropological Institute and its director, David Shankland, for the warm welcome given to the initial proposal for a Norwegian Anthropology Day, and for the excellent logistics and generous hosting during the event itself – first at the British Academy, where proceedings took place, and then in the evening at the Athenaeum Club, where the kinship of British and Norwegian anthropologies was duly demonstrated and celebrated.

An arrangement like this, including the requisite protocol and planning, requires close attention to detail. In this the RAI's Amanda Vinson joined David Shankland in providing a firm, long-term logistical anchorage on the British side of the North Sea, for which our profound thanks are due. One of the editors (Edvard Hviding) would also like to thank the other (Synnøve Bendixsen) for being the equivalent Bergen-based Norwegian anchorage, taking care of such things as organizing the smooth transport to London of a substantial proportion of Norway's institutional anthropological practitioners, and taking care of the perfect Bloomsbury accommodation of said practitioners.

This book, and the Norwegian Anthropology Day, were programme components (and are outcomes) of the project 'De-naturalizing difference: challenging the production of global social inequality', funded for 2012–2016 by the Research Council of Norway under the programme ISP-ANTRO (Institution-based Strategic Projects, grant no. 222823). We are grateful to the Research Council of Norway for the opportunities offered by this grant, and for covering the expenses relating to the events that took place in London in 2015. We also express our gratitude to the RAI for additional contributions towards the total cost of Norwegian Anthropology Day, and to the University of Bergen's Department of Social Anthropology for its contribution towards the costs of publishing this book.

In London, Dame Marilyn Strathern generously took on the unenviable job as the event's roving observer-listener and closing discussant. The spirited remarks she gave at the day's end were so inspiring, and drew together so well the many strands of the presentations, conversations and exchanges we had all participated in, that we saw it as mandatory to have the sound recording transformed into text. We are deeply grateful to Dame Marilyn for agreeing to have this text of her closing discussion published here as Chapter 9, with only very minor revisions.

In Bergen, as our editorial process has evolved, Miriam Ladstein has provided expert assistance as our copy-editor, as the able handler of a long and continuing series of revisions from the authors and as the transcriber of the original sound recording of the panel discussion and closing comments.

As organizers of the day and editors of the book, we wish finally to express our deep gratitude to all the contributors to this volume. The authors of the main chapters originally prepared their presentations for the event, and subsequently revised – and in some cases elaborated and expanded on – these texts into the final chapters in dialogue with us. The panellists also mostly arrived in London with brief prepared interventions, but were then spurred on by the mood of exchange and ended up giving longer spontaneous statements, as reflected in Chapter 8 of this book. Thank you to all of the contributors, for your energy, insights, patience and loyalty throughout the book project.

Synnøve K.N. Bendixsen and Edvard Hviding, Bergen

Contents

Chapter 1   **Portrait of a young discipline?**   1
             Synnøve K.N. Bendixsen and Edvard Hviding

Chapter 2   **Social anthropology in Norway**   16
             A historical sketch
             Olaf H. Smedal

Chapter 3   **The fieldwork tradition**   34
             Signe Howell

Chapter 4   **No direction home?**   42
             Anthropology in and of Norway
             Halvard Vike

Chapter 5   **Norwegian anthropology and development**   60
             New roles for a troubled future?
             Gunnar M. Sørbø

Chapter 6   **The unbearable lightness of being ...**   73
             a public anthropologist in Norway
             Thomas Hylland Eriksen

Chapter 7   **Disagreement, illumination and mystery**   86
             Towards an ethnography of anthropology in Norway
             Synnøve K.N. Bendixsen

Chapter 8   **Norwegian Anthropology Day**   100
             Panel discussion

Chapter 9   **Norwegian anthropology**   132
             Towards the identification of an object
             Marilyn Strathern

Contributors   137

Index   138

Portrait of a young discipline?

Synnøve Bendixsen and Edvard Hviding

✦

Preamble

This book is part of the Royal Anthropological Institute (RAI) series of volumes on national traditions of anthropology, and is the result of an invitation from the RAI to organize a 'Norwegian Anthropology Day' in London. The following chapters, including the edited transcript of a lively debate and Marilyn Strathern's thoughtful closing remarks, derive from that event, held on 30 October 2015.[1] In recent years the RAI has organized a series of annual full-day presentations of other countries' anthropological traditions (the RAI Country Series) as conveyed by speakers and panels from the countries in question: France (2013), Poland (2014), Norway (2015) and Austria (2016). In connection with the Norwegian Anthropology Day, it was noted by the RAI how:

> Norway has a distinct and diverse anthropological tradition with close ties
> to the institutions and practices of British social anthropology, and contact
> between colleagues, research centres and departments in our two countries
> is long-standing, diverse and enduring. Social anthropology in Norway is
> of significant strength in terms of national institutions and international
> presence. The global fieldwork record remains strong, there is a long record
> of public engagement by anthropologists, and employment opportunities are

---

1   See   www.therai.org.uk/events-calendar/eventdetail/308/-/norwegian-anthropology-day (accessed 23 June 2020) for the original programme and overview.

diverse. It is therefore of particular interest to have Norwegian anthropology broadly presented and discussed in dialogue among a diverse range of Norwegian practitioners and British colleagues.

We take these observations as a basic rationale for the Norwegian Anthropology Day and for this resulting volume. However, the background to organizing the event had another important element to it, which is tied up with the specificity of social anthropology as a discipline as practised in Norway. The event in London was an integral component of a major four-year collaborative research-and-outreach project involving two dozen anthropologists from the University of Bergen, the University of Oslo and the Bergen-based Chr. Michelsen Institute, entitled 'Denaturalizing difference: challenging the production of global social inequality' (DENAT).

As is further described by Bendixsen (this volume), this project was itself the result of an international audit-oriented evaluation of nine research units and eighty-eight researchers in Norwegian anthropology (Hastrup *et al.* 2011), emerging from a particular configuration of audit and funding cultures in Norway's national research system. DENAT was an 'institution-based strategic project' (ISP) and gathered its participants with the aim of developing new theoretical insights, from comparative analysis of ethnographic materials, into urgent challenges of our time, notably the diversity of global social inequality. In this sense DENAT was the institutional response of the University of Bergen to the evaluation panel's report, and was funded by the Research Council of Norway (RCN) as a direct follow-up to the international evaluation.

How the evaluation panel's conclusions led to the RCN's recruitment of a rapid follow-up committee, which in turn gave recommendations for targeted research funding to meet challenges set by the evaluation, and how this funding was announced and led to a handful of project grants, is a separate story in itself worthy of anthropological analysis (see Bendixsen, this volume). Suffice it to say that while the evaluation panel expressed some misgivings concerning the international visibility of Norwegian anthropology, the anthropologists of Norway responded by, for example, organizing the RAI's Norwegian Anthropology Day to boost that visibility – a neat convergence of supply and demand, in that the RAI was already recruiting 'national anthropologies' for its Country Series.

Institutions, trajectories, histories

Anthropology as a discipline has neither a single point of origin nor followed a single line of development (Eriksen 2008). Some have understood the history of anthropology as a discipline in terms of centres, or central traditions (e.g. Cardoso de Oliveira 2000), contrasting 'Western' anthropologists, whose topics of research interests were societies abroad, with 'non-Western' anthropologists who studied 'at home'. In Norway, however, anthropology's trajectory has been more complex: while Norway is geographically situated in 'the West', it is located at the periphery; the discipline was institutionalized by people who had been trained in the centre (the United States and Britain), but since its early days Norwegian anthropology has focused both on minorities 'at home' (the indigenous Sámi, and more recent migrant populations), while also holding in high esteem the practice of conducting fieldwork abroad, far and wide.

Norwegian anthropology was institutionalized and professionalized from the 1950s onwards by Fredrik Barth and his colleagues and associates, not least the 'Loft crowd' at Oslo's Ethnographic Museum.[2] During the 1960s and 1970s, social anthropology was institutionalized in Norway in the form of university departments. The first was founded by Fredrik Barth at the University of Bergen in 1962, as an annex to the Department of Philosophy, and heralded the emergence of a Norwegian 'social anthropology' in contrast to 'ethnography'. The department began to exist in its own right in 1965. Meanwhile at the University of Oslo, a proper department had been in place since 1964, but under the 'ethnography' label, which remained until 1987 when it was replaced by 'social anthropology', by then the mainstream Norwegian term. When the University of Tromsø was founded in 1972, (social) anthropology was from the start integral to a research group on Sámi studies, and with the gradual employment of several professors and associate professors Tromsø emerged as Norway's third consolidated anthropology centre. Meanwhile a fourth department of social anthropology was founded at the University of Trondheim in 1975 by the psychologist-anthropologist Jan Brøgger, who had previously worked with the anthropologists in both Oslo and Bergen.

Norsk Antropologisk Forening (Norwegian Anthropological Association) was formally constituted in 1980 as a means of connecting academic anthropologists with increasing numbers of qualified practitioners working outside universities in a plethora of professions. With the sheer number of trained anthropologists escalating, the association launched the journal *Norsk Antropologisk Tidsskrift* in 1991, which soon became fully peer reviewed and a strong platform for anthropology in the Norwegian language. The Norwegian Anthropological Association has also continued to organize an annual conference open to all anthropologists in Norway (and to others who would like to attend an anthropology conference where the language is Norwegian), which in recent decades has alternated between the cities of the discipline's four departments. Meanwhile, smaller groups of academic anthropologists

---

2   For a more extensive discussion, see Smedal (this volume).

have emerged at regional colleges and at institutions that in have recent years become Norway's 'new universities', but the four original departments remain the only ones that offer full state-accredited anthropology programmes.

While being a young discipline in institutional terms, anthropology in Norway goes back further in time. There were doctoral students in social anthropology prior to 1962. Johannes Falkenberg began studying ethnography in 1936 at the University of Oslo, then Norway's only university (see Smedal, this volume). As with other students, Falkenberg came to anthropology/ ethnography from archaeology, and as a young student he gained his first impressions of the discipline when Malinowski visited the University of Oslo and gave lectures. Much earlier, Knut Leem published an ethnographic account of the Sámi in 1767, and there were also pioneering nineteenth-century intellectuals with scholarly interests in the Sámi as well as in rural populations more generally. Notably, Eilert Sundt (1817–1875), a theologian and sociologist (or perhaps proto-anthropologist), wrote many books about rural ways of living (particularly in what was then the remote northern parts of Norway) as well as about communities of Romani travellers, and more specifically about food habits, costumes, marriage patterns and other topics including sex and morality (Eriksen 2018).

Such were anthropology's beginnings in Norway. But as a discipline, anthropology in Norway, however, radically shifted away from its initial 'ethnological' phase. From the 1950s onwards, Norwegian anthropology became a British-influenced 'social anthropology', much inspired by what were to become Fredrik Barth's models of 'transactionalism' or 'generative process analysis' (see Smedal, this volume). This period of growth was defined by anthropologists who pursued fieldwork both in faraway places and in different social contexts in Norway. In contrast to France, where the discipline developed regularized, strong links with museums (Chevalier 2015), the role of museums has been more limited in Norway, although Fredrik Barth and others that were part of 'the Loft crowd' used the Ethnographic Museum's attic as a location in which they could study social anthropology through the works of Radcliffe-Brown, Malinowski and others. Arne Martin Klausen was one of the few of that generation whose research interests leaned towards museum collections and material culture. In his thesis on Dayak basket ware, he used the early Norwegian ethnographer Carl Lumholtz's material from Borneo, and was inspired by Franz Boas's published lectures on 'primitive art', given in Oslo in the 1920s. Later, Klausen further developed an interest in cultural understandings and constructions of 'images' of Norway and Norwegian-ness, heading a large study on the cultural dimensions of the 1994 Winter Olympics in Lillehammer (Klausen 1999).

During the 1960s, the new department in Bergen enjoyed visits from several renowned anthropologists of the time, many of them British, including Edmund Leach, Raymond Firth, Gerald Berreman, Laura and Paul Bohannan, Adrian Mayer, Peter Worsley and John Barnes, who gave seminars and participated in workshops. In 1967, the department held a symposium, sponsored by the Wenner-Gren Foundation, on how to study the social organization of cultural difference. During the seminar, discussions on how to clarify the then blurry term 'ethnic group' emerged (Jakoubek and Budilová 2018). From this symposium came a slim edited volume that became one of the most influential books to have come out of Norwegian anthropology, *Ethnic Groups and Boundaries* (Barth 1969). Modestly published by the small Norwegian University Press, the book's success came as somewhat of a surprise to its authors (Jakoubek and Budilová 2018; see also Wu and Weller 2019). The volume's long-standing contribution to the study of ethnicity was the analytic shift away from 'objectively defined' cultural features of ethnic groups to the cultural features considered meaningful by people themselves in terms of identity and belonging. The book's contributors collectively argued that ethnic identity is self-ascribed as well as ascribed by others; it is situational; and it is defined through people's relations to others – that is, in terms of social boundaries (see also Eriksen and Jakoubek 2018). For example, the chapter by Harald Eidheim (1969) on Sámi–Norwegian relations on the Finnmark coast, inspired by Goffman (1959), argued how in a mixed Norwegian and coastal Sámi population of northern Norway the identity as Sámi was 'stigmatized' and therefore undercommunicated in inter-ethnic public situations. Conversely, Sámi identity tended to be 'overcommunicated' in private settings. The contributions represented a step away from the contemporary idea of 'cultural wholes', and Barth's interest in the study of social process (rather than cultural meaning) was evident. The project as a whole was inspired by the Manchester School of social anthropology (Max Gluckman, J. Clyde Mitchell and A.L. Epstein) and the work of Edmund Leach, although the term 'ethnicity' had not been in their vocabulary (Jakoubek and Budilová 2018). Later, Barth contributed to the anthropology of knowledge, or 'what a person employs to interpret and act on the world' (Barth 2002:1). Based on the fieldwork he had carried out in various places, particularly New Guinea and Bali, Barth pursued a comparative approach to the study of knowledge and its role in human life.[3]

Innovations in the discipline also occurred outside the established university departments. Of note here is Marianne Gullestad, who worked

---

3   For an extensive discussion of Barth's work, see Eriksen and Jakoubek (2018) and Wu and Weller (2019).

at the Oslo-based Institute for Social Research (ISF), and later also at the University of Tromsø (from 1998). Gullestad's focus on Norwegian everyday life, life histories and home (Gullestad 1984, 1997), and on racial and national boundary constructions, both of which she studied in order to understand the relation between minorities and the majority population in Norway (Gullestad 2002), brought forth the analytical term 'equality as sameness'. Drawing on the work of Louis Dumont, Gullestad's approach to egalitarianism in Norway suggested that being considered as similar in social interaction is a prerequisite for being treated as an equal, and this brings along certain expectations on how newcomers should adapt to everyday life in Norway. The concept of 'equality as sameness' is considered essential to understanding the enactment of 'Norwegian-ness' and remains a continuing point of discussion in Scandinavian anthropology more widely (see e.g. Bendixsen *et al.* 2018; Bruun *et al.* 2011; Vike *et al.* 2001).

A large number of scholars and their contributions could have been mentioned in this short introduction, but this would not be the full story. We do not wish to draw up a directory of anthropologists in Norway during the twentieth and twenty-first centuries, but rather cast some light on some of the processes, directions and roads created, taken and followed by social anthropology in Norway. This portrait of a discipline located on the 'periphery', but always connected to the 'centre', is but partial and remains simply a preliminary sketch. The following chapters will refine this sketch, further rounding out a picture of Norwegian anthropology.

The chapters

The historical trajectories of Norwegian anthropology are laid out in elaborate detail by Olaf Smedal in Chapter 2. The relatively unknown Jens Kraft published a volume of ethnographic research in 1760, in which he discussed similarities in the cultural behaviour and institutions of separate groups of 'savage peoples', and there were notable successors to this work, such as the explorer-ethnographer Carl Lumholz. Meanwhile, it took quite some time before ethnographically inclined students could be taught and supervised: not until the late 1940s were such opportunities offered by professors at the Ethnographic Museum in Oslo. When Fredrik Barth returned from the University of Chicago in 1949 and later obtained a doctorate from Cambridge, he brought with him the first wave of post-war anthropological theory, eagerly welcomed by young scholars in the reading room they had set up in the museum's loft, and who were at the time starved of modern anthropological scholarship.

Following on from the political shifts that unfolded during the 1960s, critical assessments were made of Barth's theoretical approach, which was criticized for being too focused on economic rational man, for pursuing 'methodological individualism' and for being ahistorical. Inspired by Marxist-oriented work during the 1970s and 1980s, research appeared on work, class and gender. Simultaneously, anthropologists also turned to the study of groups in Norway that were not indigenous like the Sámi, but to marginal 'outsider groups' or ethnic minorities established through immigration. This boosted the profile of fieldwork 'at home', which had long been common anyway, ever since the 1950s 'period of frugality'. Funding for long-term fieldwork in remote places had remained rather limited, and so working in Norway had not been seen as inferior. It was only later that fieldwork 'at home' became considered as perhaps a 'second-best' option to fieldwork afar. Smedal concludes his chapter by looking at contemporary studies in an age of globalization.

The 'Loft crowd' at the Ethnographic Museum in Oslo discussed by Smedal also plays a prominent role in the next chapter, by Signe Howell. Howell considers the trajectories of ethnographic fieldwork in the two main academic institutions in Norwegian anthropology: the departments in Oslo and Bergen. She gives insights into how changing structures of academic degrees and evolving ideas of anthropological knowledge production have shaped the practice of fieldwork, particularly in temporal and spatial terms: for how long it is undertaken, and how far away. Howell sketches an intellectual terrain in which advantageously positioned and publicly renowned individuals with ethnographic interests coexisted with colleagues who in simpler ways aspired to do 'exotic fieldwork', but with little actual collaboration or conversation between these two groups them. Norwegian approaches to fieldwork from the 1950s until the 1970s must be understood partly as a consequence of the early anthropologists' commitment to developing anthropological theory, strongly influenced by Fredrik Barth's approach to fieldwork: the purpose of fieldwork was tightly connected to its capacity for providing ethnography to test a specific theory, rather than collecting detailed materials for the sustained, holistic analysis of culture and society. This theoretical slant also partly explains why fieldwork among researchers from Norway was generally conducted for shorter periods of time when compared to those from the UK: while in British departments fieldwork was generally expected to last for eighteen months, around nine months was the norm in Norway.

During the 1960s and 1970s, Norwegian anthropology was also defined in terms of the somewhat disparate intellectual environments in Bergen and Oslo. While Bergen was shaped by Barth's leadership and a focus on transactionalist analysis (the 'Bergen School'), with an increasing range of collaborative projects, anthropologists in Oslo were more individualist, intellectually diverse and involved in fewer projects, which in turn created a more heterogeneous theoretical foundation there. This, however, has changed. In the twenty-first century, many major collaborative projects have been developed in Oslo, while Bergen has long since abandoned the practice of following a single theoretical model. The two departments are similar in terms of how fieldwork remains prioritized, and even master's students are required to carry out six months of mandatory fieldwork. This methodological hallmark of anthropology has been saved, as it were, from the excesses of neoliberal university reforms.

In Chapter 4, Halvard Vike sets out to deconstruct the metaphor of 'doing anthropology at home', arguing that by producing a distinction between 'home' and 'not home', anthropologists reproduce 'the savage slot' (Trouillot 1991), and (re)establish the idea of a homogeneous nation-state in which what anthropologists 'share' with people or groups living in that nation-state is taken for granted. Discourses about the risk of 'home blindness', tied up with presumptions of familiarity, are both explicit and implicit in various understandings of what 'good anthropology' in Norway should look like. This has contributed to continued constructions of otherness, and to presumptions of a (Norwegian) nation defined by a homogeneous culture, while little anthropological attention has been drawn to the study of institutions, bureaucracy and policies in Norway. The sharp distinction made between fieldwork at home and abroad draws on a presumption that a so-called radical alterity is necessary to produce anthropological knowledge, and that doing fieldwork 'at home' is fundamentally different from doing fieldwork in a context that is 'not home'. Vike proposes an alternative approach: we need to give proper attention to how social positionality enters our research process, and thus reflect on how we think about and conceptualize culture – which should be understood as a social process of construction, not as a pattern of more or less completed form. Fieldwork necessitates involvement, and the relationship between the anthropologist and those being studied can include different types of alterities.

Vike writes against the idea that anthropologists require radical alterity in order to understand the way in which culture is generated. Instead, he notes how the distinction made between fieldwork 'at home' and 'afar' ignores the fact that any analytically fruitful application of the idea of culture must rest on the acknowledgement that, first, culture is a fundamentally relational concept (which thus involves the anthropological self) and, second, that 'the invention of culture' is fundamentally involved in the social practice of attributing meaning to social processes. He shifts our attention to the need to better understand the relevance of our own social positionality as researchers regardless of where 'the field' is situated. The relevant question concerning fieldwork is not whether it is done at home or abroad, but rather one of epistemology and relationality.

In Chapter 5, Gunnar M. Sørbø discusses a different, but equally important, aspect of Norwegian anthropology's public relevance: its consistent dialogue with, and applicability in, the massive and diverse field of Norwegian development assistance and aid projects. Since the 1960s, Norwegian anthropologists, particularly in Bergen and originally spurred on by Fredrik Barth, have conducted fieldwork in parts of the world where issues of development aid and challenges of conflict and instability have loomed large. Sørbø takes as his example the situation in Sudan, the locale of his own long-term research, but also a place in which generations of younger scholars have become engaged in generating anthropological understandings of conflict and inequality, the role of development aid, and regional social and political dynamics. At the meeting point between being applicable (though not necessarily applied), methodologically rigorous and theoretically innovative, Norwegian anthropological scholarship since the late 1960s has contributed to advancing methodological approaches that can be applied to complex practical problems, and improve development policy and practice. Some early anthropologists, including Barth, believed that anthropology's particular ability to move between micro and macro scales of economy and society was well-suited to generating a better understanding of the dynamics of undesirable dimensions of social life – knowledge that could in turn be applied to help reduce or remove such dynamics.

These early endeavours led to long-standing and ongoing collaboration with the University of Khartoum, as well as the participation of Norway (together with the United States and the UK) in the peace process in Sudan. The Sudanese case demonstrates the ability of the anthropological discipline to pursue basic, applied and policy-oriented research simultaneously. It also shows how the anthropologist can (and should) move between different scales of empirical observation and analysis. Relevant investigative scales of analysis and the question(s) to be posed must be discovered empirically, which increases the recognition that any explanation of a given social dynamic will depend upon the scale of the analysis chosen. Since the mid 1980s, as policy has focused on questions concerning conflict and development has moved towards macro-political developments and good governance, political scientists have gained more ground in the Norwegian 'development scene', while anthropologists have been marginalized and have become to some degree less visible in Norway. In this context, Sørbø urges anthropologists to recognize their abilities to integrate different levels of analysis. Cooperation with other disciplines must be encouraged, and anthropologists' own ability to attend to issues at different scales must be strengthened: 'There is clearly no "correct" scale for an investigation of, say, conflicts in Darfur, but there may be an appropriate one for answering different [types of] questions'.

In Chapter 6, Thomas Hylland Eriksen discusses Norwegian anthropology's prominent public presence. He describes the risks involved in contributing to the public sphere with anthropological knowledge, concepts and perspectives, while nevertheless insisting on anthropology's necessity, both in terms of remaining relevant and in terms of the responsibility anthropologists have to the people among whom they work. While anthropology does not have a 'societal assignment' in the way sociology and political science do, remaining within the university's ivory tower is ultimately untenable since it means withholding knowledge that society has funded, and it generates greater distance between the public and academics. That said, not all intellectuals need to be of the public sort: 'Without the often arcane and difficult original research that never travels beyond seminar rooms and online university libraries, public anthropologists would have nothing to be public about'.

Public anthropology in Norway is described as a diverse arena. Thematically, its contributions consist, on the one hand, of light-hearted takes on such phenomena as graduation celebrations and particular food habits, and on the other, approaches to the societal and cultural logics behind racism, female circumcision and patriarchy. In a more complex way, light-hearted comments about serious matters can gain the public's attention but, at the same time they may obscure the serious intentions behind messages. The impact of public anthropology on one's academic career can also be risky as too much public visibility can lead to colleagues' scepticism vis-à-vis one's theoretical contribution to the discipline. Eriksen further notes that the translation of academic terms and insights unfamiliar to non-anthropologists in presenting relevant anthropological knowledge should not be taken lightly. With regard to translation, Eriksen writes from his own experience of being misinterpreted by the right-wing extremist who massacred people at Utøya and in central Oslo in July 2011. Eriksen had long spoken in public of the need to 'deconstruct the majority' from an anthropological position, whereas he was misinterpreted by the right wing in Norway and labelled as a traitor. Nevertheless, in light of the need for anthropology to continue to show its multifaceted 'relevance', Eriksen encourages public anthropologists to keep their message simple and to foster the public's imagination, without thereby oversimplifying.

In Chapter 7, Synnøve Bendixsen draws on ethnographic methods and anthropological models – the very tools of our discipline – to cast a bright light on the 'inner practices' of anthropology in Norway. As a partial outsider who has been mostly trained abroad, she is well positioned to observe the 'customs' of the 'particular group of people' known as 'anthropologists in Norway'. Bendixsen examines these people's relations of production through glimpses of everyday practice and key rituals of 'the group', and she introduces the reader to debates concerning the hegemony of audit culture and evaluation in Norwegian academia. She identifies distinctive patterns of local knowledge built by Norwegian anthropologists in the past, present and future, considers their domestic and international relations, and pays particular attention to the resilient tradition of long-term fieldwork, held in high esteem over several generations.

Dialogues: panel discussion

Towards the end of this book, we offer readers something special: an edited, shortened transcription of the lively, moderated panel discussion that unfolded during the course of the Norwegian Anthropology Day. Brief presentations were given by nine representatives of Norwegian anthropology within and outside academia, along with some PhD candidates and master's students, as well as by colleagues from British anthropology. The panel was designed to tease out particular epistemological and political configurations of anthropology in Norway, and to examine differences and similarities between Norwegian and British anthropological practice. Panellists were requested both to present statements and reflections from their own particular perspectives, and to comment directly on particularly relevant positions and arguments in the presentations that form the book's central chapters. We believe that this part of the book captures and retains the spirit of the moment as it unfolded on the day.

Closing remarks

As the organizers of Norwegian Anthropology Day, we were privileged to welcome Marilyn Strathern as the day's 'roving observer'. She had generously agreed to provide some final comments based on closely following the day's proceedings. Although there was no intention that her remarks would be written up, it was fortunate that a sound recording was made (in conjunction with the panel discussion). Strathern's closing remarks were marvellously perceptive, and traced the narratives and trajectories of the entire day in a clear-cut presentation that was part chronological and part analytical, and pulled together the day's diverse strands of thought and narrative in an original set of observations, propositions and conclusions. The closing remarks given by Strathern are reproduced here in a manner similar to those of the panel discussion, as a lightly edited transcription, but in this case not shortened. Thus the day ended on a most inspirational note.

Scene-setter: betwixt and between

The outline we have given of the book's six main chapters brings forth the question of what, if anything, is the relevance of the specifically national frame for better understanding anthropology in Norway? Is there (still) a particularly Norwegian social anthropological tradition? Following institutional expectations and global tendencies, scholars in Norway are increasingly prioritizing publications in English, and an increased number of courses in university undergraduate and postgraduate programmes are offered in English.

Much social anthropology in Norway has been strongly influenced by British social anthropology. It has been playfully suggested that Norwegian anthropologists see themselves as 'the matrilateral relatives of their British colleagues (with Barth playing the part of the mother's brother)' (Eriksen 2008:170). Theoretically, however, Norwegian anthropologists have been more wide-ranging than many of their British counterparts (or relatives). Furthermore, the following chapters draw attention to two distinctive aspects of social anthropology in Norway: the particular kind of public role taken by anthropology along with its applicability; and how, ever since the beginnings of the discipline, anthropologists have pursued fieldwork both 'at home' in Norway and 'afar'. We close our introduction and set the scene for the chapters by focusing more closely on these two distinctive, but clearly interrelated dimensions.

In November and December 1979, Fredrik Barth entertained (and enlightened) the Norwegian public on what was then the only available TV station (the state-funded NRK) with a four-episode series called *Andres Liv – Og Vårt (Others' Lives – And Ours)*.[4] The series was introduced as a TV programme that considered distant and nearby ways of living 'as perceived and experienced by social anthropologist Fredrik Barth'. Striking in his informality of appearance, as a modest but learned professor with a mane of flowing grey hair, Barth looked into the camera from behind his desk at the Ethnographic Museum and talked about his extraordinary range of fieldwork experiences from around the globe, while showing black-and-white and colour slides of those very places and the people there (for which he had to draw the curtains in his old-style museum office). Through this and other engagements with the broader public, Barth became a sort of enlightenment figure in Norway (Vike, this volume).

Later, other public intellectuals, notably Arne Martin Klausen and Thomas Hylland Eriksen, continued to close the gap between academic anthropology and anthropology in the public sphere by providing commentary and expertise to help bring about insights that could contribute to social reform

---

4   The TV series. originally broadcast as four episodes of about 25 minutes each, is available at the NRK website, https://tv.nrk.no/serie/andres-liv-og-vaart/1979/FOLA01004679/avspiller.

and improved policy. Since the 1990s, many recognized anthropologists have been called upon by journalists for interviews and comments on TV and radio, and many more have been invited to speak to municipalities, schools, NGOs, parliamentary committees and other types of forum – and on a vast repertoire of topics (food, sport, environmentalism, Islamism, right-wing movements, irregular migrants, climate change and more). Other anthropologists are called on for their expertise on the perhaps 'exotic' ethnography of certain regions of the world – sometimes by the media and sometimes by the government, including the foreign service.

While all this brings along challenges for anthropologists, who 'have to be able to switch between a playful mode exploring options and lifeworlds, and a serious concern with the plight of homeless heroin addicts' (Eriksen, this volume), it also means that over the years the public has become quite familiar with anthropology's perspectives, approaches and forms of knowledge. The strong public position of anthropology in Norway, compared to the situation in many other countries, is not only connected to its media presence and to giving public talks, of course. It is also integrally linked to its societal relevance as research that may be driven by curiosity at the outset but attains particular relevance in applied and policy-oriented contexts (Sørbø, this volume). A consistent observation among Norway's anthropologists is that one never knows when a particular, perhaps remote, part of the world may gain prominence on the public sphere or in government ministries, but what is certain is that anthropologists with long-term fieldwork experience in those places will be asked to provide commentary and informed advice when the need arises.[5]

The second and final point, that since the discipline's inception Norwegian anthropologists have pursued fieldwork in Norway and abroad, with quite a few continuing to do both, is also worth elaborating. Norwegian anthropology has a long-standing tradition of producing thorough and holistic ethnography based on protracted, often repeated, periods of fieldwork, and the collective Norwegian anthropological research record in this sense covers most parts of the world. While not confined to Norway, this particular tradition of anthropological practice, often developing long-term familiarity with societies through repeated periods of fieldwork (e.g. Howell and Talle 2012), provides the ground for engaging in rethinking and theorizing globally diverse forms of social inequality, an issue which has been an enduring focus of research and teaching at the national level.

---

5   For a more extensive discussion of the many-stranded approaches to engaged public anthropology in Norway and Scandinavia more generally, see Bringa and Bendixsen (2016).

Perhaps the tradition of simultaneously pursuing fieldwork in Norway and abroad is due, in part, to the particular position Norwegian anthropology holds in terms of centre/periphery relations. Anthropologists in Norway have engaged in diverse ways with theoretical approaches prevalent at the 'centre' (the UK and the United States, but also France) while also responding to – embracing in some cases, rebuffing in others – theories advanced within Norway, such as those that emerged from 'the Bergen school' in the 1960s, but also later initiatives seen either as 'fads' or as great advances. Norwegian anthropologists have also recognized Norway as a relevant ethnographic field of study, always with new empirical and analytical challenges, while also pursuing fieldwork overseas, studying topics and locations as diverse as ethnic conflict and war in Sudan and Bosnia and cosmology and climate change in the Pacific. This diversity in research can be invariably found in any of the country's four anthropology departments. Perhaps Norwegian anthropology is thus first and foremost characterized by taking a 'betwixt and between' position, identifying itself as situated neither at the centre nor at the periphery, which is a position from which it has thrived.

References

Barth, F. 2002. 'An anthropology of knowledge'. *Current Anthropology* 43(1):1–18.

——— (ed.). 1969. *Ethnic Groups and Boundaries*. Oslo: Universitetsforlaget.

Bendixsen, S., Bringslid, M.B. and Vike, H. (eds). 2018. *Egalitarianism in Scandinavia: Historical and Contemporary Approaches*. London: Palgrave.

Bringa, T. and Bendixsen, S.N. (eds). 2016. *Engaged Anthropology: Views from Scandinavia*. New York: Palgrave-Macmillan.

Bruun, M., Jakobsen, G. and Krøijer, S. 2011. 'Introduction: the concern for sociality practicing equality and hierarchy in Denmark'. *Social Analysis* 55(2):1–19.

Cardoso de Oliveira, R. 2000. 'Peripheral anthropologies "versus"' central anthropologies'. *Journal of Latin American Anthropology* 5(1):10–30.

Chevalier, S. (ed.) 2015. *Anthropology at the Crossroads: The View from France*. Canon Pyon: Sean Kingston Publishing.

Eidheim, H 1969. 'When ethnic identity is a social stigma'. In F. Barth (ed.), *Ethnic Groups and Boundaries*, pp. 281–97. Oslo: Universitetsforlaget.

Eriksen, T.H. 2008. 'The otherness of Norwegian anthropology'. In A. Bošković (ed.), *Other People's Anthropologies*, pp. 169–85. Oxford: Berghahn Books.

——— 2018. 'Anthropology, Norway in'. In H. Callan (ed.), *The International Encyclopedia of Anthropology*, pp. 4359–75. New York: Wiley.

Eriksen, T.H. and Jakoubek, M. 2018. 'Introduction: Ethnic groups, boundaries and beyond'. In T.H. Eriksen and M. Jakoubek (eds), *Ethnic Groups and Boundaries Today: A Legacy of Fifty Years*, pp. 1–19. London: Routledge

Goffman, E. 1959. *The Presentation of Self in Everyday Life*. New York: Anchor Books.

Gullestad, M. 1984. *Kitchen-Table Society: A Case Study of the Family Life and Friendships of Young Working-Class Mothers in Urban Norway*. Oslo: Universitetsforlaget.

——— 1997. 'A passion for boundaries: reflections on connections between the everyday lives of children and discourses on the nation in contemporary Norway'. *Childhood* 4(1):19–42.

——— 2002. 'Invisible fences: egalitarianism, nationalism and racism'. *Journal of the Royal Anthropological Institute* 8(1):199–226.

Hastrup, K., Garsten, C., Hansen, T.B., Mitchell, J.P. and Vuorela, U.M. 2011. 'Social and cultural anthropological research in Norway: an evaluation'. Oslo: Research Council of Norway, Division of Science.

Howell, S. and Talle, A. (eds). 2012. *Returns to the Field: Multitemporal Research and Contemporary Anthropology*. Bloomington: Indiana University Press.

Jakoubek, M. and Budilová, L. 2018. 'Fredrik Barth and the study of ethnicity: Reflections on ethnic identity in a world of global political, economic and cultural changes'. In T.H. Eriksen and M. Jakoubek (eds), *Ethnic Groups and Boundaries Today: A Legacy of Fifty Years*, pp. 187-212. London: Routledge.

Klausen, A.M. (ed.). 1999. *Olympic Games as Performance and Public Event: The Case of the XVII Winter Olympic Games in Norway*. New York: Berghahn.

Trouillot, M.R. 1991. 'Anthropology and the savage slot: the poetics and politics of otherness'. In R.G. Fox (ed.), *Recapturing Anthropology*, pp. 17–44. Santa Fe, NM: School of American Research.

Vike, H., Lidén, H. and Lien, M. (eds.) 2001. *Likhetens paradokser (The paradoxes of egalitarianism)*. Oslo: Universitetsforlaget.

Wu, K. and Weller, R.P. (eds). 2019. *It Happens among People: Resonances and Extensions of the Work of Fredrik Barth*. New York: Berghahn.

2

Social anthropology in Norway

A historical sketch

Olaf H. Smedal

❖

Even if one goes about it in a chronological manner, it is not immediately obvious where an account of the history of social anthropology in Norway should begin. But one thing is clear: to assume that 'anthropology' begins with the establishment of university departments containing that word in their names would be a mistake. As is the case in other European nations, much of what later became 'anthropological research' was handled by museum personnel, who received artefacts, specimens and reports submitted by explorers, adventurers and of course missionaries. In Norway's case, fewer artefacts were submitted by colonial officers, of which Norway had very few.

Hence, although a number of Norwegians were recruited by trading companies in their heyday, such as the Danish East India Company and the Danish West India Company, this is something on which the present chapter does not capitalize. Norwegians prefer to think that their ancestors played no part in the imperialistic extravaganzas that marked many European nations and, although we have reluctantly come to realize that we are less than innocent in this regard, most of us tend to point out instead that Norwegians themselves were colonized for well over 400 years (by the Danes from 1380 to 1814). The fact that Norwegian ship owners and sailors busied themselves for one and a half centuries with the lucrative slave trade (Gøbel 2011) is something to which average members of the Norwegian public give little thought. They may be vaguely aware of the former Danish-Norwegian colonies in the West Indies, which are nowadays attractive tourist destinations, but Danish-Norwegian exploits in 'the East', such as the Trankebar colony (1620–1845) on the Indian sub-continent, are only slowly becoming common public knowledge – largely thanks to a book that was published at the turn of the millennium (Ustvedt

2001).[1] A more recent scholarly exposition of Norwegian forays – to Africa and the Pacific in this case (Kjerland and Bertelsen 2015) – long after the union with Denmark had ceased to exist, should debunk once and for all any lingering ideas that Norwegians, as 'noncolonial colonials' (Bertelsen 2015:4, 7, 22–3), did not involve themselves in imperialistic exploits and atrocities.

However, space is limited, and given the aims of this volume I suspect there is less interest in how collections of material object and assorted notes from distant lands were handled in museums in Oslo (then Christiania), Trondheim, Tromsø and Bergen in the nineteenth century than in what most readers will think of as social anthropology in its modern sense.[2] By this I mean the discipline that came into its own in the early twentieth century and is associated with long-term fieldwork, preferably based on information acquired through the local vernacular. The major reference here is of course Malinowski, whose first chapter on field research methods in *Argonauts of the Western Pacific* (Malinowski 1922:1–20) is still taught in some courses in Norway, but Radcliffe-Brown should also get a mention, even if he is far less often taught nowadays.

The teachings of these revolutionaries – anti-evolutionists and anti-diffusionists as they were – had little impact on those few Norwegians who pursued a career in ethnographic museums, however. In fact, probably the best-known of these 'proto-anthropologists', Carl Lumholtz (1851–1922), was trained as a theologian and could more accurately be described as an explorer (see Howell, this volume).

1　'Denmark–Norway … was an early modern multi-national and multi-lingual real union consisting of the Kingdom of Denmark, the Kingdom of Norway (including Norwegian overseas possessions Faroe Islands, Iceland, Greenland, et cetera), the Duchy of Schleswig, and the Duchy of Holstein. The state also claimed sovereignty over two historical peoples: Wends and Goths. In addition, the state included colonies: St. Thomas, St. John, St. Croix, Ghana, Tharangambadi, Serampore, and Nicobar Islands. The state's inhabitants were mainly Danes, Norwegians and Germans, and also included Faroese, Icelanders and Inuit in the Norwegian overseas possessions, a Sami minority in northern Norway, as well as indigenous peoples and enslaved Africans in the colonies. The state's main cities were Copenhagen, Christiania (Oslo), Altona, Bergen and Trondheim. The state's primary official languages were Danish and German.' 'Denmark–Norway', *Wikipedia*: en.wikipedia.org/wiki/Denmark%E2%80%93Norway (accessed 29 September 2019).

2　The ethnographic collections in Oslo date back to 1857; in Trondheim, they can be traced to the establishment of the Royal Norwegian Society of Sciences and Letters in 1767. In Bergen, what is now the University Museum opened in 1825; in Tromsø, the ethnographic collection dates to 1872.

Before I come to modern, fieldwork-based anthropology, however, I should mention very briefly a far less well-known figure than Lumholtz: Jens Kraft, who was born in Norway in 1720, but raised in Denmark, where he died forty-five years later.[3] At twenty-six, he was appointed professor of philosophy and mathematics at Sorø Academy – an institution of higher learning established in 1586.[4] The reason Kraft deserves a place in this account is that, besides writing learned books on physics as well as metaphysics, he also published a volume in Danish in 1760 on the 'contrivances, customs and opinions of savage peoples for the enlightenment of human origins and progress in general', which later translated into German and Dutch (Kraft and Høiris 1997; see also Klausen 1999). This book, according to anthropologist Pia Bennike:

> may have been the first ethnographic world survey. In it, Kraft noted the
> similarity in cultural behavior and institutions in widely separated groups,
> which led him to postulate that all human beings shared the same mental
> processes – an idea that was to echo throughout nineteenth-century
> anthropology.
>
> (Bennike 1997:330)

As a curiosity, given the preoccupations in certain corners of recent anthropology, I note that, according to the English language Wikipedia entry on Kraft, who was clearly a polyglot extraordinaire, he 'introduced the study of ontology to Scandinavian academic circles'.[5]

Turning now to the goings-on at the Ethnographic Museum in Oslo, it had its own professors, who were obliged to take on a student whenever, once in a blue moon, one knocked on their door. These professors, such as Yngvar Nielsen (1843–1916), Ole Martin Solberg (1879–1946), Nils Lid (1890–1958) and Gutorm Gjessing (1906–1979), were historians, ethnologists/folklorists, geographers or archaeologists. They were effectively sidelined in what was known as 'ethnography', and lectured at odd intervals (if at all) on what were known as the Lapps (that is, the Sámi) or read aloud from compendia that they had produced by abbreviating foreign-language ethnographies. What these professors invariably told their students was that while they were welcome to study the discipline, they could forget about ever getting any kind of gainful

---

3   See 'Jens Kraft', *Wikipedia*: en.wikipedia.org/wiki/Jens_Kraft (accessed 29 September 2019).

4   See 'Sorø Academy', *Wikipedia*: en.wikipedia.org/wiki/Sorø_Academy (accessed 29 September 2019).

5   Quoted from 'Jens Kraft', *Wikipedia*: en.wikipedia.org/wiki/Jens_Kraft (accessed 26 August 2020).

employment from it.[6] Many years later, one of those students (and one of my first teachers) commented that the professorial lectures were so boring that he and his fellow students actually took turns at showing up: to abandon the seminar room completely would be tantamount to a boycott, which they deemed to be too cruel (Harald Eidheim, cited in Eriksen 2008a:181).

Such was the situation a few years after the Nazi occupation of Norway (1940–1945) had ended and reconstruction was under way, which was when the teenager Fredrik Barth entered the University of Chicago. Three years later, he returned to Norway as a 20-year-old with a master's degree in anthropology, 'just married and out of work' (Eriksen 2015:12). He rapidly gravitated to the Ethnographic Museum, where he met with the professor and his by then handful of turn-taking students, a group that soon came to be known as 'the Loft crowd' because they occupied rooms adjoining the library on the top floor.

The Loft crowd

The arrival of Barth in 1949 was – according to every member of the Loft crowd who has ever spoken about it later – electrifying; as one of them said, 'he came into the attic like a whirlwind' (Eriksen 2015:13). He was younger than them but he already had a degree, and he brought the freshness of the great academic outdoors with him, arriving straight from the United States. What may surprise some readers is that when he began to enlighten the students in the museum reading room, he preached the gospel according to Radcliffe-Brown.[7] But the students – most of whom were to prove their professors wrong, in that they did secure positions in academia – were regularly left to their own devices when Barth was off to do fieldwork, either in Norway, where he did his first stint, or in Kurdistan. Next, he spent a year at the London School of Economics, where he met and learned from Edmund Leach while writing up his material on the Kurds. However, when Barth submitted his monograph to the University of Oslo, in submission for a doctoral degree, he was turned down (Barth 2007:3). The committee, being unfamiliar with what was entailed

---

6 Harald Eidheim remembered Gutorm Gjessing telling him, 'if you want to come here and study, fine. But don't you believe you'll ever get a job in that profession' (quoted in Eriksen 2008a:180). Gjessing, who trained as an archaeologist, held the chair at the Ethnographic Museum from 1947 to 1973. In an interview, Axel Sommerfelt recalled similar remarks: '"Yes, it would be nice to get a student here", [Gjessing said], "but you'll never get anything to do! There are four positions in the country, and they're all taken by young men, so you'll be on your own!"' (quoted from Simonsen and Flikke 2009:265).

7 According to Axel Sommerfelt, 'Fredrik was a strong supporter of Radcliffe-Brown' (quoted from Simonsen and Flikke 2009:265).

in writing a doctoral dissertation in anthropology, contacted Evans-Pritchard, asking what such a process looked like in Oxford. Evans-Pritchard replied that one would need a minimum of one year of fieldwork. Since Barth could boast barely half as much, the conclusion was foregone. The work was published (Barth 1953), but the 23-year-old had to embark on another field research trip – this time to the Swat valley in Pakistan – and write up that material before he was awarded his doctorate in 1957 by Cambridge University, to which Leach had by then migrated. The published version of Barth's doctoral dissertation, *Political Leadership among Swat Pathans* (1959), quickly established him as a leading anthropologist of his generation.

But back to the Loft. Barth was instrumental in bringing the exciting new work of the first wave of post-war anthropologists to the attention of the Loft crowd, and he found time, too, to guide each one in getting their own material into shape. Gjessing, the professor at the time, did not like it much; in his view, theory was just a fad. In his defence, however, it must be said that the Loft students were free to conduct their own seminars, and he allowed them to buy all the literature that they needed.[8] In the end, they got their qualifying degrees and, as just mentioned, one by one almost all of them managed to find teaching jobs or secure funding for new research. Thus, the Loft crowd – of whom some remained in Oslo, while others relocated temporarily or permanently elsewhere – is really at the core of social anthropology in Norway as we know it, and it is fair to say that all of its members were deeply influenced by Barth's rapidly gelling vision of what anthropology is – and how one goes about conducting an anthropological investigation.

While the Loft crowd's influence on Norwegian anthropology was decisive over the decades to come, Barth's teaching also went down very well with a curator at the Ethnographic Museum: Johannes Falkenberg (1911–2004). Falkenberg's studies in ethnography began in 1936, and he conducted his first

---

8   Johannes Falkenberg recalled, 'When Malinowski's opinions began to take hold, Solberg [the professor] snorted and called him an à la mode author with the observational powers of a tourist. The ethnologist Nils Lid was equally averse to theory. He edited the publications of the Norwegian Ethnological Society and said outright that heavy-handed theoretical musings went straight into the trash can' (quoted in Larsen 1981). Meanwhile, Axel Sommerfelt has stated, 'We were largely self-taught because Gjessing was not obligated to lecture us. He lectured two hours a week, and they were spent on the geographers. We attended those lectures, but it was only for so long that we could attend geography lectures for undergraduates. ... But we held seminars, and we created an environment that partly undermined what Gjessing wanted us to do. He thought we had blinkers because we specialized in social anthropology of the British variety' (quoted from Simonsen and Flikke 2009:265).

fieldwork in 1938 among the Sámi in Finnmark, northern Norway, on the basis of which he received his qualifying degree (see Falkenberg 1941). But when, five years after the end of the Second World War, the opportunity presented itself for fieldwork further afield, he and his wife departed for Australia. Reading up before the trip, he was struck by the clarity of Radcliffe-Brown's analyses of Aboriginal social organization (Radcliffe-Brown 1931), and in fact it was Falkenberg who introduced Radcliffe-Brown to the nascent milieu of modern anthropologists in Norway. But he admitted that the Loft crowd actually became his teachers; they embodied a combination of irreverence and a critical attitude that Solberg simply lacked (Larsen 1981).

Falkenberg's study (1962) of the Port Keats Aborigines, originally published in 1950, received a rave review by Rodney Needham (1962b).[9] Needham, notorious for his vicious polemics (see e.g. Needham 1962a), was exceedingly enthusiastic about Falkenberg's monograph. The book, he said:

> has no theoretical pretensions (it lacks even a solitary reference to Lévi-Strauss or Leach) and expressly abstains from comparative considerations; [Falkenberg] has instead patiently unearthed and clearly reported an astonishing range and unexpected wealth of fascinating detail, and it is evident that at every point in his researches he asked just the right factual questions and went to conscientious and protracted pains to establish reliable answers.
>
> (Needham 1962b:1316)

Praising Falkenberg's detailed account of ceremonial exchange, Needham sums up by simply saying, 'This is real ethnography'. He continues:

> The same standard of precision is maintained as the author proceeds to discuss totems, sex groupings, age-grades, moieties, sub-sections, and the individual. At this point it has to be confessed, and with good reason in this case, that it is really impossible to do justice in a review to a work of this scope and character.
>
> (ibid.:1317)

The commendations simply go on and on until Needham concludes:

> ... it does not take $500,000 (for example) to produce work of this quality, and even such huge amounts cannot in themselves procure it.

---

9   Lévi-Strauss, too, reviewed the book very favourably (Lévi-Strauss 1963).

Money, after all, is not the chief obstacle, and the quality of Falkenberg's
brilliant monograph indicates in itself that the real difficulty is to find
anthropologists half as able as he is.

It can be only very rarely that a reviewer lays down a book with such
a grateful sense of satisfaction and admiration as Falkenberg's remarkable
ethnography inspires.

(ibid.:1318)

Falkenberg is explicit that his own study is fundamentally inspired by
Radcliffe-Brown.[10] However, in his second book, co-authored with his wife
Aslaug (Falkenberg and Falkenberg 1981), Falkenberg remarks that Radcliffe-
Brown actually had it all wrong (Larsen 1981). Here, Falkenberg explains
that precisely because he was so overwhelmed by Radcliffe-Brown's lucid,
functionalist analyses in descent theory mode, he had, unfortunately, found
himself tweaking the evidence in the direction of descent theory:

A general reluctance not to be in harmony with Radcliffe-Brown's theories
caused us to present a somewhat distorted picture of the kinship system and
the local organization among the Aborigines at Port Keats.

(Falkenberg and Falkenberg 1981:68).[11]

Reconsidering the original material, then, the authors concluded that the
primary concern of Port Keats Aboriginals is the dynamics of affinity and
alliance – not descent.[12]

Establishing departments

Having sketched some of the early post-war developments in social
anthropology in Norway, I now turn to the political and budgetary realities of
things, namely academic institutions. Throughout the 1950s there really was
only one place where modern social anthropology was taught and discussed,

---

10   Ironically, Needham was later to castigate Radcliffe-Brown's work on Australian
     Aborigines (see Needham 1974).
11   Falkenberg spoke less diplomatically when he was interviewed in Norwegian:
     'I used pliers and a sledgehammer, by fair means or foul, in order to fit my
     observations into his framework' (*Og jeg brukte tang og slegge og list og lempe for å
     passe mine observasjoner inn i hans ramme*) (quoted in Larsen 1981).
12   From what I have been able to establish, Falkenberg's theoretical about-turn was
     received with less praise, although his superb powers of observation and the
     diligence of his (and his wife's) reporting were still lauded (Fuary 1983; Rumsey
     1982; Testart 1983).

if only at the graduate level, and that was the Ethnographic Museum. But in 1960 the University of Oslo embarked on a series of reforms, one outcome of which was to establish an introductory programme of study in ethnography, and in 1964 a proper department (or institute) was established, which retained 'ethnography' in its name, a situation that did not change until 1978, when 'social anthropology' replaced it.

However, the University of Oslo had been beaten, for what was soon to become the Department of Social Anthropology at the University of Bergen had already come into being in 1962 – as an annex of the Department of Philosophy – and once again Barth was centre stage. Attempts at securing a tenured readership for him in Oslo had been unsuccessful.[13] Thanks to deft lobbying by Henning Siverts, Barth, having just turned down an offer from Columbia University, arrived and set up shop. Siverts was one of the Loft crowd, and had relocated to the Bergen University museum, and for his lobbying efforts he was nicknamed St Henning the Baptist because he heralded the coming of the Saviour.[14] As far as Bergen is concerned, the rest, as they say, is history. I shall return to one detail shortly, but let me just mention another point here: one of the first things Barth did in Bergen was to instigate a research project that was to culminate in the publication of a small book on entrepreneurs and social change in northern Norway (Barth 1963).[15]

Ten years later, in 1972, the University of Tromsø was inaugurated, and although no social anthropology department was established, what was

---

13   Clearly, Barth the anthropologist had no ally in Gjessing the ethnographer, but the readership in question was allocated to the Faculty of Humanities, and the weight of historians may have been decisive (see Eriksen 2015:66).

14   Or, in the words of Ottar Brox: 'it was a liberating revelation to attend seminars in Bergen and be confronted with Barth's naturalism. What had been chaotic and incomprehensible became clear and transparent, and those of us who were recruits experienced the encounter with the Bergen milieu as if we were led out of the desert with Barth in the role of Moses' (Brox 1998).

15   Here is Barth's explanation for this: 'I regarded it as basic to the nature of anthropology to do cross-cultural and international research, so my task was to create a greater public appreciation of the enormous value and contemporary relevance of active international research. But I also needed to promote empirical work within Norway because showing this form of relevance was no doubt important to the general reception of anthropology there. Taking my brief from the Tavistock Institute in London and their industrial studies of task organization in coal mining in England, I launched a study of task organization in herring fishing with purse seines along the west coast of Norway and also a cooperative study of the role of entrepreneurs in social change in northern Norway' (Barth 2007:7).

there from the very start was a research group for Sámi studies, which soon developed into a stable group of anthropologists organized in various ways over the decades that followed.

Finally, in 1975, at what is now the Norwegian University of Science and Technology in Trondheim, a department of social anthropology was established. Here, as well as in Tromsø, Barth-trained anthropologists were appointed from the word go. But the students in Trondheim were obliged to take their exams in Bergen well into the 1980s,[16] suggesting that in some circles the Bergen department retained its status as the Holy See of Norwegian anthropology long after Barth had left it.

Since 1975, then, full study programmes in social anthropology have been running continuously in Oslo, Bergen, Trondheim and Tromsø, and to the best of my knowledge no one has so far suggested establishing a fifth programme. In what follows, I dwell a little on the Tromsø department, whose mandate differed from that of the others.

Tromsø anthropology – and the Sámi

While ethnographic research in Tromsø had long been centred at the city's museum, the appointment of anthropologists at the new university signalled changing times. For one thing, the entire institution was expected to prioritize research pertaining to northern Norway and the education of its population. The region suffered from a brain drain, and many of those from the region who 'went south' (geographically speaking) for higher education never returned. Thus, the University of Tromsø – located some 400 kilometres north of the Arctic Circle – is not an educational institution like any other: from its inception it was a political project. Accordingly, the anthropologists who were hired were expected to concentrate their efforts on social phenomena in that northern area. Cue the Sámi.

Precisely because the university was established with the explicit aim of developing local knowledge, what for all practical purposes later became a department of social anthropology began as a unit for Sámi studies. Therein lay a certain dynamic, not to say dynamite: how can one conduct unbiased research on the Sámi – an aboriginal people having suffered first the Norwegian state's neglect and then, much later, its aggressive 'Norwegianization' – if one's fundamental identity is Norwegian? And how should self-identifying Sámi students deal with the fact that their teachers tended to be not only ethnic Norwegians but also southerners? It is difficult to convey briefly to an international audience the difficult and sensitive minority

---

16 Harald Aspen, personal communication, 22 October 2015.

situation of the Sámi in the early 1970s, but the work of Harald Eidheim on Sámi impression management is helpful (Eidheim 1969; see also Eidheim 1971).

Ten years later, things escalated: the Norwegian Parliament decided to push ahead with its plans for constructing a hydroelectric dam across the Alta river, flooding natural habitats as well as Sámi camping grounds, and, it was argued, jeopardizing Sámi reindeer husbandry and salmon fishing. This brought things to a head. Ethnopolitics threatened to become a household word as Sámi activists went on hunger strike on the lawn in front of the Norwegian Parliament, and prominent professors and many of their students from Oslo and elsewhere travelled to the site where the dam was to be built and chained themselves to rocks, being finally dragged away by the largest call-out of police since the end of the Second World War (Ramstad and Saugestad 2015:100). Sámi activists also occupied the office of the prime minister, Gro Harlem Brundtland. These situations and events, in the sense deployed by the Manchester School (Gluckman 1940; Kapferer 2005), were both revealing and transformative. What began as an environmental protest shape-shifted into a struggle for the fundamental rights of an indigenous people, as chronicled by Robert Paine (1982).[17] Thus, although the dam was finally built, 'the Alta case' led to greater Sámi self-rule and awareness of the Sámi situation. As a result, 1989 saw the establishment of the Sámi Parliament of Norway, and in 1997 King Harald proclaimed that the Kingdom of Norway had been established on the territory of two peoples, the Norwegians and the Sámi (Ramstad and Saugestad 2015:101).

In fact, in 1968 several Norwegian anthropologists had already taken a strong interest in advocating for what became known as 'collective human rights', and they were instrumental in founding the International Work Group for Indigenous Affairs (IWGIA), whose headquarters are located in Copenhagen.[18] Since then, a steady trickle of Norwegian anthropology students and tenured professors alike has voluntarily given their labour to the organization.

While a concern for the rights of indigenous groups has been an enduring feature of Norwegian anthropology, this concern merged with other activities. Interestingly, the specific topics for research conducted by the Loft crowd over the years varied considerably. These include: social organization in Africa and the anthropology of law (Axel Sommerfelt); Sámi–Norwegian ethnic

---

17 In 1998, Paine was awarded an honorary doctorate by the University of Tromsø.

18 Helge Kleivan, one of the Loft crowd members, moved to Copenhagen in 1966 and was a founding member of IWGIA, which he was to head from its inception until his death in 1983. See Dahl (2009) for a detailed account of the IWGIA's first forty years.

relations and Caribbean matrifocality (Harald Eidheim); the symbolism of basket ware in Borneo, Norwegian foreign aid, media studies and the 1994 Winter Olympics in Lillehammer (Arne Martin Klausen); Inuit in Canada and Greenland (Helge Kleivan); folk music and folk dance in Norway and Jamaica, as well as linguistic code switching in northern Norway (Jan-Petter Blom); rhetoric, political organization and drinking patterns in Chiapas (Henning Siverts); and household organization in northern Norway, followed by long-term economic change in a fishing community and in the cloth trade in Malaysia (Ingrid Rudie). Moreover, as the educational programmes became formalized and the number of graduate students and tenured staff began to grow, something that Synnøve Bendixsen takes up in her contribution to this volume, a corresponding pluralism of fields of study became evident.

Signe Howell (this volume) addresses the role that fieldwork has played in Norwegian anthropology, so I shall show some restraint here, but if one looks at the lists of submitted master's and doctoral theses in Norway, the close to 2,500 titles so far evince great variety with respect to topic, location and theoretical bent.

A-changing times

A question I should address, however, is how the departments differed from each other in terms of theoretical orientation from the time they were established until well into the 1980s. From what I have been able to glean from some of my elders, Barth's enthusiasm and charismatic style of instruction were infectious, and his students, some of whom soon became his colleagues, saw little reason to depart from the path the master had laid out. The result was a fairly homogeneous professional atmosphere both in Bergen and in Oslo until the radicalization that took place in Europe in the late 1960s also spread to Norwegian universities. This radicalization of students in particular – sparked off, as I remember it, by the US military adventures in Southeast Asia – was helped along in the anthropology departments by theoretical work by French anthropologists, particularly scholars such as Maurice Godelier, Claude Meillassoux and Emmanuel Terray, as well as by Maurice Bloch from his base at the LSE and Jonathan Friedman from – it seemed – several places at once. Readers will recall that in this literature Karl Marx appeared in the list of references with some frequency.

Integral to this student radicalization was the fact that Norway was preparing for its first referendum since 1926 (which ended prohibition), namely over Norway's membership of the European Economic Community (EEC), the precursor of the European Union. Exemplifying what one of my colleagues (Tord Larsen) once referred to as 'the Norwegian package syndrome' (Larsen 1984), it was impossible to be in favour of Norway's membership of the EEC if one was already against US warfare in Vietnam. And if that was one's view of things, and one was an anthropology student, then one was also already committed, even if one did not yet know it, to denounce Barth's theoretical programme as it was laid out in, for example, 'Models of social organization' (Barth 1966), a work that 'can be conceived as marking a "paradigm" shift in British social anthropology' (Kapferer 1976:2).

This meant that many students and some of the scientific staff in Oslo took it upon themselves to demonstrate how Barth's programme was deficient. I think what irked the critics most was the combination of three features: first, the 'rat choice', utilitarian, economic man, games theory tone of exposition; second, the declared bottom-up analytical strategy that, to many, simply said 'methodological individualism'; and third, the apparent lack of concern with history, with the workings of big systems and powerful structures (capitalism, imperialism) and the exploitation of the poor by the rich. In short, what Barth was doing was bourgeois science, doomed to liberate no one.

Of course, when Robert Paine published a critique of Barth's models (Paine 1974), these critical, local voices received a powerful ally. And that was the year Barth moved from Bergen to Oslo to take up the vacant professorship – not in the University of Oslo's Ethnographic Institute but rather at the Ethnographic Museum.[19]

As an aside, Tim Ingold (2013), relates how, as a graduate student, he had fallen under the spell of Barth's 'transactionalism', as it was known in the English-speaking world – Norwegians have always known it as 'generative process analysis' – and had spent a few months in Bergen, as he puts it, to 'soak up the heady atmosphere [Barth] had created there' before departing for fieldwork among the Skolt Sámi in Finland. Upon his return to Bergen sixteen months later (in late 1972 or early 1973), Ingold found that 'the paradigm in which [he] had placed so much faith was on the verge of collapse' (ibid.:8). The times were indeed a-changing.

A proper analysis of this change must wait for another occasion, but I think that concomitant with it were specifiable shifts in Norway's political and economic situation: the feminist movement of the early 1970s was gaining strength (resulting in important welfare reforms), Norway's 'no' to EEC membership in 1972 (which still stands, even after a second referendum

---

19 For an illuminating account of the life and times of the Ethnographic Museum – both prior to and subsequent to Barth's decade there (he resigned in 1985 upon having been awarded one of the rare 'lifetime' government grants bestowed on those whose work the Norwegian Parliament deems essential for society at large) – see Bouquet (1996).

in 1994) and the fact that Norway became an oil-producing and exporting country.

So, what happened next? Before I answer that question, I should mention one publication specifically because it did something that had not really been done before. What I have in mind is the volume edited by Arne Martin Klausen on Norwegian 'culture in action' (Klausen 1984), which concerned itself with how ethnic Norwegians of no particular creed, age, orientation or location go about things; in short, what makes common, 'unmarked' (Gullestad 1991:4) Norwegians tick.

Of course, Norwegian anthropologists had been working in Norway and on Norwegians for decades already – not only on the Sámi, but on ethnic Norwegians as well. In fact, when my own studies began in the early 1970s, most of my teachers had conducted fieldwork in Norway – finding it practically impossible during the first decade or so after the Second World War to secure grants for international travel, they had no choice – or were soon to embark on such fieldwork. Barth's (1963) volume on the role of the entrepreneur is a case in point. Thus, the familiar sighs from students that fieldwork 'at home' would be considered second-best (not 'real' anthropology) is something that, for my generation, had little basis in reality.[20] That prominent anthropologists such as Marilyn Strathern (1987) and Kirsten Hastrup (1991) were later to cast doubt on the very possibility of doing 'anthropology' in the researcher's 'own' 'culture' (the use of scare quotes here being a nod to the subheadings in Hastrup's subversive critique of, especially, Marianne Gullestad's work) was something that concerned us only in passing.[21]

The various chapters in the collection edited by Klausen range widely. One sets out to analyse the Norwegian mind set in general – this is the chapter already alluded to, which presents the odd, syllogistic-like classificatory links that prefigure one's opinions on practically everything under the sun. And interestingly, two of the chapters were penned by people born and raised outside Norway: the Argentinian Eduardo Archetti and the South African Julian Kramer – both of them by then long-term residents in Norway. There

---

20 Such suspicions are, however, reinforced by works such as Gupta and Ferguson (1997).

21 Discussions over the possibility of being (or not being) a 'native anthropologist' have not ended. See Gefou-Madianou (1993), Kuwayama (2004) and Peirano (1998). In Norway in 1991, just when the Norwegian higher education system was accepting hordes of new students, including onto the anthropology programmes, Cato Wadel, one of the first students to be taught in Bergen, published a textbook on anthropology 'at home' (Wadel 1991), which has been reissued and amended a number of times. The book is quite popular among students regardless of whether or not it is on their reading lists.

is no space here to summarize the different chapters, but I think it is easy to underestimate the book's impact – not on the Norwegian general public, which is still largely oblivious to its existence – but on many anthropology students who suddenly had liberating thought that one was not obliged to study out-groups, ethnic minorities or people in extreme conditions in order to do good anthropology. An excellent example of such work is Marianne Gullestad's study of young working-class mothers (Gullestad 1984).

Be that as it may, what did happen next? The Marxist-oriented anthropology of the 1970s and early 1980s, which inspired much research on peasants (of which there appeared to be many, including in Norway) and modes of production, households and the sexes – which was, in short, research on work, class and gender – gave way to perspectives attributable to the hermeneutically informed (and much less politically oriented) writings of Clifford Geertz. But although reading Geertz's fluent prose came as a relief to many students after having struggled with the dryer texts of British anthropologists (and Barth),[22] and the patently more tortuous ones by the French (at least in English translations), they found his style was difficult to emulate. And for those of us who had begun to see that the world consisted of more than class struggle and false consciousness, Pierre Bourdieu seemed to provide what was missing: a clear view of how agents, now also agents in the bodily sense, went about making the best of whatever their circumstances permitted, while simultaneously affirming, by way of habituated strategies, those very same circumstances. Less suddenly, but by no means less decisively, Marilyn Strathern's work was beginning to appear on reading lists.

Could one, then, speak of an anthropology with a specifically Norwegian flavour? As is well known, similar questions have been asked about anthropology in other nations as well (see e.g. Bošković 2008; Fahim 1982; Gerholm and Hannerz 1982; Gullestad 1989; Peirano 1998). More likely than not, answers to such a question will lead to debate. Perusing the chapters in this volume, readers might be able to formulate their own answer, or perhaps they will just

---

22 This parenthesis complements Eriksen's assessment: 'When I studied at Oslo in the early 1980s, the entire pamphlet [Barth's 'Models of social organization'] was read by first-year sociology students, while the social anthropology students only had to read the first chapter, the one on transactions. It was one of the first texts I read as a sociology student, and to those of us who had begun to grow accustomed to the student-friendly, almost chatty style in much of the curriculum, the encounter with Barth's dry, concise writing came as a shock. That text offered nothing but a promise of hard work … [It] was his most ambitious theoretical text, and it may seem as if Barth made an effort to write it out without a superfluous word. In this he doubtless succeeded, but as a result students had to attack it with hammer and chisel.' (Eriksen 2015:92).

agree with what some people think: that Norwegian anthropology is largely a branch of the anthropology developed in Britain or, even more narrowly, that it is but 'a subsidiary of Oxbridge' (Eriksen 2008b:170).

Finally, and to conclude by posing a second question: What might the future of our discipline be in Norway? Recalling that Foucault once 'described anthropology and psychoanalysis as being the two disciplines that cut across the entire field of the social sciences while at the same time residing at its periphery' (Godelier 2000:303), one might hope that even if social anthropology's demise in the metropolitan centres were to occur, its subsumption under programmes such as 'global studies', for example, would mean that it will have all the brighter prospects in the world's peripheries.

We would be happy if it were so.

Acknowledgements

I wish to thank Sidsel Saugestad for providing me with the manuscript of an article she wrote with Jorun Bræck Ramstad before it appeared in *Norsk Antropologisk Tidsskrift* (Ramstad and Saugestad 2015) and Anne Kathrine Larsen for digging up hard-to-find information on the Department of Social Anthropology at the Norwegian University for Science and Technology. Thanks also to Tord Austdal, Tone Bringa, Are Knutsen and Synnøve K.N. Bendixsen, and to the latter for alerting me to Jens Kraft and the article about him by Arne Martin Klausen (1999).

References

Barth, F. 1953. *Principles of Social Organization in Southern Kurdistan*. Oslo: Universitetets Etnografiske Museum.

——— 1959. *Political Leadership among Swat Pathans*. London: Athlone Press.

——— 1966. 'Models of social organization'. Occasional Paper No. 23. London: Royal Anthropological Institute.

——— 2007. 'Overview: sixty years in anthropology'. *Annual Review of Anthropology* 36:1–16.

——— (ed.). 1963. *The Role of the Entrepreneur in Social Change in Northern Norway*. Bergen: Universitetsforlaget.

Bennike, P. 1997. 'Demography: Denmark'. In F. Spencer (ed.), *History of Physical Anthropology: An Encyclopedia*, vol. 1, pp. 330–34. New York: Garland Publishing.

Bertelsen, B.E. 2015. 'Introduction: Norwegians navigating colonial orders in Africa and Oceania'. In K.A. Kjerland and B.E. Bertelsen (eds), *Navigating Colonial Orders: Norwegian Entrepreneurship in Africa and Oceania*, pp. 1–37. Oxford: Berghahn Books.

Bošković, A. (ed.). 2008. *Other People's Anthropologies: Ethnographic Practice on the Margins*. Oxford: Berghahn Books.

Bouquet, M. 1996. *Sans og Samling ... hos Universitetets Etnografiske Museum/ Bringing It All Back Home ... to the Oslo Ethnographic Museum*. Oslo: Universitetsforlaget.

Brox, O. 1998. 'Fredrik Barth fyller 70 år' [Fredrik Barth turns 70]. *Dagbladet*, 20 December. Available at: www.dagbladet.no/kultur/fredrik-barth-fyller-70-ar/65495198 (accessed 29 September 2019).

Dahl, J. 2009. 'IWGIA: a history'. IWGIA Document No. 125. Available at: www. iwgia.org/images/publications/0015_IGIA_-_a_history.pdf (accessed 29 September 2019).

Eidheim, H. 1969. 'When ethnic identity is a social stigma'. In F. Barth (ed.), *Ethnic Groups and Boundaries: The Organization of Cultural Difference*, pp. 39–57. Oslo: Universitetsforlaget.

——— 1971. *Aspects of the Lappish Minority Situation*. Oslo: Universitetsforlaget.

Eriksen, T.H. 2008a. 'Akademisk ambivalens: Harald Eidheim intervjuet av Thomas Hylland Eriksen' [Academic ambivalence: Harald Eidheim interviewed by Thomas Hylland Eriksen]. *Norsk Antropologisk Tidsskrift* 19:177–88.

——— 2008b. 'The otherness of Norwegian anthropology'. In A. Bošković (ed.), *Other People's Anthropologies*, pp. 169–85. Oxford: Berghahn Books.

——— 2015. *Fredrik Barth: An Intellectual Biography*. London: Pluto Press.

Fahim, H. (ed.) 1982. *Indigenous Anthropology in non-Western Countries*. Durham, NC: Carolina University Press.

Falkenberg, A. and Falkenberg, J. 1981. *The Affinal Relationship System: A New Approach to Kinship and Marriage*. Oslo: Universitetsforlaget.

Falkenberg, J. 1941. *Bosetningen ved Indre Laksefjord i Finnmark: Optegnelser fra 1938* [Habitation at Inner Laksefjord in Finnmark: records from 1938]. Oslo: Etnografisk Museum.

——— 1962. *Kin and Totem: Group Relations of Australian Aborigines in the Port Keats District*. Oslo/London: Oslo University Press/Allen and Unwin.

Fuary, M.M. 1983. Review of Falkenberg and Falkenberg (1981). *Mankind* 14(2):148–9.

Gefou-Madianou, D. 1993. 'Mirroring ourselves through Western texts: the limits of an indigenous anthropology'. In H. Driessen (ed.), *The Politics of Ethnographic Reading and Writing*, pp. 160–81. Saarbrücken: Verlag Breitenbach.

Gerholm, T. and Hannerz U. (eds). 1982. 'The shaping of national anthropologies'. *Ethnos*, special issue, 47 (1/2).

Gluckman, M. 1940. 'Analysis of a social situation in modern Zululand'. *Bantu Studies* 14(1):1–30.

Gøbel, E. 2011. 'Danish shipping along the triangular route, 1671–1802: voyages and conditions on board'. *Scandinavian Journal of History* 36(2):135–55.

Godelier, M. 2000. 'Is social anthropology still worth the trouble? A response to some echoes from America'. *Ethnos* 65(3):301–16.

Gullestad, M. 1984. *Kitchen-Table Society: A Case Study of the Family Life and Friendships of Young Working-Class Mothers in Urban Norway.* Oslo: Universitetsforlaget.

——— 1989. 'Small facts and large issues: The anthropology of contemporary Scandinavian society'. *Annual Review of Anthropology* 18:71–93.

——— 1991. 'Studiet av egen samfunnskultur som utfordring' [The study of one's own culture as a challenge]. *Norsk Antropologisk Tidsskrift* 2:3–9.

Gupta, A. and Ferguson, J. 1997. 'Discipline and practice: "The field" as site, method, and location in anthropology'. In A. Gupta and J. Ferguson (eds), *Anthropological Locations: Boundaries and Grounds of a Field Science*, pp. 1–46. Berkeley: University of California Press.

Hastrup, K. 1991. 'Antropologiske studier af egen kultur' [Antropological studies of one's own culture]. *Norsk Antropologisk Tidsskrift* 2:10–14.

Ingold, T. 2013. 'Anthropology beyond humanity'. *Suomen Antropologi* 38(3):5–23.

Kapferer, B. 1976. 'Transactional models reconsidered'. In B. Kapferer (ed.), *Transaction and Meaning: Directions in the Anthropology of Exchange and Symbolic Behavior*, pp. 1–22. Philadelphia: Institute for the Study of Human Issues.

——— 2005. 'Situations, crisis, and the anthropology of the concrete: the contribution of Max Gluckman'. *Social Analysis* 49(3):85–122.

Kjerland, K.A. and Bertelsen, B.E. (eds). 2015. *Navigating Colonial Orders: Norwegian Entrepreneurship in Africa and Oceania.* New York: Berghahn.

Klausen, A.M. 1999. 'Jens Kraft: Norsk filosof og antropolog fra 1700-tallet' [Jens Kraft: Norwegian philosopher and anthropologist from the eighteenth century]. *Norsk Antropologisk Tidsskrift* 9:168–9.

——— (ed.). 1984. *Den Norske Væremåten* [Being Norwegian]. Oslo: Cappelen.

Kraft, J. and Høiris, O. 1997 [1769]. *Kort Fortælling af de Vilde Folks fornemmeste Indretninger, Skikke og Meninger, til Oplysning af det menneskeliges Oprindelse og Fremgang i Almindelighed* [A brief chronicle of the noblest arrangements, customs and opinions of savage peoples, for the illumination of the origin and general progress of humanity]. Aarhus: Invention Press.

Kuwayama, T. 2004. *Native Anthropology: The Japanese Challenge to Western Academic Hegemony.* Melbourne: Trans Pacific Press.

Larsen, T. 1981. 'Johs fyller 70' [Johs turns 70]. *Antropolognytt* 3(1). Available at: http://antropologi.org/faghistorieprosjekt/johannes-falkenberg/ (accessed 29 September 2019).

——— 1984. 'Bønder i byen' [Peasants in town]. In A.M. Klausen (ed.), *Den Norske Væremåten* [Being Norwegian], pp. 15-44. Oslo: Cappelen.

Lévi-Strauss, C. 1963. Review of Falkenberg (1962). *L'Homme* 3(3):133–4.

Malinowski, B. 1922. *Argonauts of the Western Pacific: An Account of Native Enterprise and Adventure in the Archipelagoes of Melanesian New Guinea.* London: Routledge.

Needham, R. 1962a. *Structure and Sentiment: A Test Case in Social Anthropology.* Chicago: University of Chicago Press.

——— 1962b. Review of Falkenberg (1962). *American Anthropologist* 64:1316–18.

——— 1974. 'Surmise, discovery and rhetoric'. In *Remarks and Inventions: Skeptical Essays about Kinship*, pp. 109–68. London: Tavistock Publications.

Paine, R. 1974. 'Second thoughts about Barth's models'. Occasional Paper No. 32. London: Royal Anthropological Institute.

——— 1982. 'Dam a river, damn a people? Saami (Lapp) livelihood and the Alta/ Kautokeino hydro-electric project and the Norwegian Parliament'. IWGIA Document No. 45. Copenhagen: International Work Group for Indigenous Affairs.

Peirano, M.G.S. 1998. 'When anthropology is at home: the different contexts of a single discipline'. *Annual Review of Anthropology* 27:105–28.

Radcliffe-Brown, A.R. 1931. *The Social Organization of Australian Tribes.* Melbourne: Macmillan.

Ramstad, J.B. and Saugestad, S. 2015. 'Samiske studier: et tidsbilde og noen analyseperspektiver' [Sàmi studies: the representation of a period and its analytical approaches]. *Norsk Antropologisk Tidsskrift* 26:92–110.

Rumsey, A. 1982. Review of Falkenburg and Falkenburg (1981). *Pacific Studies* 6(1):122–5.

Simonsen, J.K. and Flikke, R. 2009. 'Motstandskamp og fag: et intervju med Axel Sommerfelt' [Resistance and profession: an interview with Axel Sommerfelt]. *Norsk Antropologisk Tidsskrift* 20:263–77.

Strathern, M. 1987. 'The limits of auto-anthropology'. In A. Jackson (ed.), *Anthropology at Home*, pp. 16–37. London: Tavistock Publications.

Testart, A. 1983. Review of Falkenberg and Falkenberg (1981). *L'Homme* 23(1):169–71.

Ustvedt, Y. 2001. *Trankebar: Nordmenn i de Gamle Tropekolonier* [Trankebar: Norwegians in the Old Tropical Colonies]. Oslo: Cappelen.

Wadel, C. 1991. *Feltarbeid i Egen Kultur: En Innføring i Kvalitativt Orientert Samfunnsforskning* [Fieldwork in one's own culture: an introduction to qualitatively oriented social research]. Flekkefjord: Seek.

3

The fieldwork tradition

SIGNE HOWELL

Editors' note

Since her arrival in Norwegian anthropology in 1987, Professor Howell has been an indefatigable champion of global fieldwork and of the need for a thriving discipline to have continuous recruitment of new practitioners who work in localities across the world. For the Norwegian Anthropology Day she was asked to give a personal account of her continuous engagement with fieldwork – indeed with 'the fieldwork tradition' – through the changing bureaucratic structures of universities, anthropology programmes and funding schemes. The following is the personal account that Professor Howell gave, and for maximum effect and to reflect the 'moment' in October 2015 it has been left as is with only very minor editorial changes and with key bibliographic references added.

I

When I was a fresh postgraduate diploma student in social anthropology at Oxford in 1975, Wendy James gave an introductory lecture on fieldwork and its role in the discipline. Wendy had spent some time as a visiting lecturer at the University of Bergen's anthropology department, and told us in a disparaging tone of voice that, in Bergen, nine months of fieldwork was the norm. In the UK, by contrast, we were told, eighteen months were regarded as appropriate – much less than that would not enable us to gain some mastery of the language and grasp 'the natives' point of view'. Fredrik Barth's book on the Baktaman of Papua New Guinea (Barth 1975) had just been published. This was based on approximately nine months in the field. Wendy's claim seemed to be vindicated. However, in this case, let it be said, this did not detract significantly from the quality of the book. It has become a classic in the anthropology of Papua New Guinea.

I never thought much more about this. I had no plans to work in Norway. However, when I did take up a position at the University of Oslo in 1987, I began to realize that the situation was more complex than Wendy had given us to understand. This was in part owing to the particular degree structure of Norwegian universities prior to the adoption of a new PhD scheme, then followed by the Bologna regime, and partly, I suggest, due to the influence of Barth – a brilliant wizard at relatively brief fieldwork in many parts of the world. As Olaf Smedal (this volume) has told us, the influence of Barth on the young enthusiastic people gathered at 'the Loft' of the Ethnographic Museum in Oslo during the nineteen fifties, and later at the department in Bergen, cannot be exaggerated.

According to one of the Loft crowd who I talked to while preparing this text, they all dreamt of exotic fieldwork but were restrained by lack of funding. The Research Council had been established in 1949, but grants were only given to those who had completed the degree of *Magister Artium*, and which was then the qualifying degree for an academic career, and took about eight years from start to finish. For the early anthropologists who wanted the experience of exotic fieldwork, this at best would mean brief fieldwork in Norway with the Sámi. In the not-so-gentle words of Johannes Falkenberg, ethnography at the time meant 'lappology'. Alternatively, they could write a library thesis based on existing published material. Axel Sommerfelt, for example, wrote a re-interpretation of Fortes' Tallensi material (Sommerfelt 1958) before undertaking his own fieldwork in what was then Rhodesia. This meant that they were theoretically sophisticated, but had no first-hand experience of meeting the kinds of people that they had been reading about in much discussed texts by Malinowski, Radcliffe-Brown – a major influence on the early students – Evans-Pritchard, Fortes and Firth and others, as well as the Americans such as Boas and his student's.

When Falkenberg, after his *Magister Artium*, left for Australia in 1950 for nearly two years to study the Murinbata Aborigines at Port Keats (see Falkenberg and Falkenberg 1981), he was the first anthropologist to receive a scholarship from the newly established Research Council. When he returned from fieldwork, his lectures and the ensuing discussions in the Loft based on first-hand experience were, in the words of Arne Martin Klausen, one of the students at the time, 'like manna from heaven'.

The chances are that Falkenberg had read books on Australian aborigines by one of the true pioneering Norwegian amateur ethnographers, Carl Lumholtz. An early explorer with a remarkable ethnographic talent, Lumholtz collected botanical and zoological and, later, ethnographic material for a number of major museums in Europe and the United States. He started his career in 1880 when, twenty-nine years old, he set off for Australia in order to collect 'natural objects' for the Botanical Museum in Oslo. He spent more than four years in the country, getting to know the Aborigines in Queensland well, having spent more than a year living with people on the Herbert River. He published widely – on occasion sensationally – about his experiences. His first book, *Among Cannibals* (Lumholtz 1889), was translated into several languages, and made him a popular lecturer in the United States, particularly with the American Geographical Society, in whose journal he published a number of articles on social life amongst native populations, not only in Australia, but also based on subsequent travels in Mexico and Borneo. In fact, Lumholtz's two-volume account of five years spent in Mexico (Lumholtz 1902) is still highly regarded, and was republished by Cambridge University Press in 2011.

When, in 1994, two of my colleagues in Oslo, Arne Martin Klausen and Arve Sørum, put on an exhibition at the Ethnographic Museum that dealt with Lumholtz's travels, they compiled a detailed catalogue with substantial original texts by Lumholtz (Klausen and Sørum 1993). This was translated and published in Spanish by Mexico's Comisión Nacional para el Desarrollo de los Pueblos Indígenas (Klausen and Sørum 2006). At the same time, Sørum (who has undertaken long-term fieldwork in Papua New Guinea and east Indonesia) undertook to travel in Lumholtz's footsteps through Kalimantan (present day Indonesian Borneo) and made a film that was shown on Norwegian television in connection with the exhibition.

Given his early international fame, his many ethnographic texts, his wonderful photographs and the many ethnographic items that he deposited at the Ethnographic Museum, it seems curious that Lumholtz was not taken much account of by the Loft crowd. This was explained to me by one of its members by the reigning attitude at the time to ethnographic descriptions. These were, he said, of little inherent interest, but were brought to bear only in so far as someone wished to make a theoretical point. This seems rather peculiar in a country with a rich history of individuals with a strong sense of adventure and curiosity about alien parts of the world. The explorations of the Arctic and Antarctic by Roald Amundsen and Fridtjof Nansen have fired the imagination of generations of school children. Helge Ingstad's many books based on his life with indigenous peoples in Greenland, Alaska and northern Canada similarly engaged. Yet their work received scant attention by the early anthropologists. The notorious Thor Heyerdahl, who wished to be taken seriously by the Norwegian anthropological milieu, was rejected as an amateur, if not a charlatan – not least, I suspect, because of a lack of theoretical sophistication coupled with too lively an imagination. Interestingly, however, Heyerdahl provided funding for one of the students at the Loft,

Henning Siverts, to undertake his first major fieldwork in Mexico in the late 1950s (see e.g. Siverts 1960).

II

From my enquires and conversations with several of the Loft crowd and the subsequent generation of anthropologists who formed the discipline in Norway, it transpired that, while fieldwork was central to anthropological practice, fieldwork during the early days, at any rate that which was undertaken in Norway, tended to be planned in order to test a particular theory rather than with the aim of a sustained analysis of culture and society anchored in detailed ethnography. Periods in the field were also often brief. For example, Barth's fieldwork on a Norwegian fishing boat was undertaken in order to study the power game of the skipper. It lasted eight weeks resulted in his influential article 'Models of social organization' (Barth 1966). A demanding role model for his students and colleagues!

When Marianne Gullestad started her more open-ended, holistic fieldwork amongst working-class women in Bergen (see e.g. Gullestad 1984), this was dismissed as lacking in theory by the majority of those in power. She remained for a long time on the periphery of Norwegian anthropology, and never got a university appointment. Several reasons may account for this. To concentrate exclusively on studying Norwegian society in depth, not just as something to do in-between 'more important' field research in remote parts, or to prove a theoretical point, was only one of them. To focus on women may have been equally, if not more, unacceptable, especially when undertaken in an urban setting. However, Gullestad did become well-known nationally and internationally, and to undertake 'anthropology at home' became fully acceptable in the wake of her pioneering research.

I need to say a few words about the departments in Oslo and Bergen. As Olaf Smedal (this volume) has pointed out, Barth was invited to establish an anthropology department at the University of Bergen in 1962. This department and the Department of Ethnography in Oslo developed somewhat different profiles, which may have influenced the different practices of fieldwork. Bergen became under Barth a more homogeneous intellectual environment in which transactionalist analysis became the ruling dogma, leading to what was called the 'Bergen School'. Perhaps because of this unified theoretical approach, fieldwork in Bergen was organized under several regional and thematic umbrellas. Ethnicity and migration became the main foci for some time, and the academic staff organized research mainly in specific parts of the world (the Middle East and East Africa). Graduate students preparing for the *Magister Artium*, or the new *hovedfag* (a degree system more structured than the *Magister* degree) were recruited to join the teams. This led, for example, to long-lasting cooperation with the universities of Khartoum and later Juba, and many graduate students, as well as senior research fellows and Norwegian and Sudanese staff, undertook fieldwork in Sudan. It was in that connection that Wendy James met the Bergen anthropologists in Juba, and was herself invited to Bergen. This particular Bergen situation may have contributed to the nine-month fieldwork practice that Wendy mentioned to us Oxford students in 1975. Bergen anthropologists tended to focus on a delineated topic with a formulated hypothesis; they were part of a team that collaborated, and therefore, perhaps, to use interpreters or work through English appeared less problematic than it might otherwise have done. At the same time, there were in Bergen several eager individuals who set off on their own initiative for other remote places, and stayed there up to eighteen months.

In Oslo, by contrast, there were only eager individuals. No research group resembling that in Bergen was established until Thomas Hylland Eriksen became director of CULCOM in 2004. This was a major strategic cross-campus project, and initiated a large-scale anthropological study of a suburb in Oslo with a substantial immigrant population, examining issues of belonging. Otherwise, Oslo students and staff constituted a heterogeneous group of people, most of whom regarded one year as a reasonable time to stay away for one's first period of fieldwork. But this was not a requirement, and some were satisfied with six to nine months. The first woman to be appointed to any anthropology department in Norway was Ingrid Rudie. She joined the Loft crowd in 1958 and, subsequent to attaining her *Magister* degree based on fieldwork with a Sámi group (Rudie 1962), received a scholarship to go to Malaysia, where in the early 1960s she studied a fishing community (see Rudie 1994). Unusually at the time, she spent several months studying the Malay language at SOAS before setting off for a year of fieldwork. Here she met Firth who was helpful in discussing her planned fieldwork.

There was no attempt in Oslo to direct the individual choice of field site. Students went to areas that caught their imagination: to Asia, Africa, Melanesia and later – mainly due to the influence of the appointment of the Argentinian Eduardo Archetti in 1976 – to Latin America. Archetti, who had done his doctoral field research on peasant societies under the supervision of the Marxist-structuralist Maurice Godelier in Paris, brought Marxism to Oslo together with a regional interest in Latin America (see Archetti 2003; Archetti and Stølen 1975). Apart from the Marxist influence, the Oslo department did not adhere to any one theoretical school. There was a policy of letting every flower bloom. Meanwhile, the Research Council had established a small-grant programme for graduate students to undertake fieldwork overseas and this, together with fieldwork scholarships from the Institute of Comparative Cultural Research, enabled many to fulfil their dream of undertaking exotic fieldwork while still being graduate students. Following the completion of *Magister Artium* or the new *hovedfag*, ambitious students could apply for a three-year research fellowship. They were the ones who aimed for an academic career, and they mostly used the fellowship to undertake extensive new fieldwork. Most tended to return to the same country where they had undertaken their original work, but with a new thematic focus. In effect, this meant that the nine-month fieldwork standard primarily applied to those who left academia for careers elsewhere.

III

In the 1960s, 1970s and into the 1980s, very few people took a doctorate in social anthropology in Norway. For those few who did, it was more like the French *doctorat d'état* taken later in one's career than a PhD. When I arrived at the University of Oslo in 1987, my first task was to establish a structured PhD programme on top of the *Magister* and *hovedfag* degrees. This represented a major shift in research policy. The candidates selected for this new programme received what was to me, coming from the UK, and used to ESRC grants, an enormous scholarship for four years (but which included the requirement of some teaching). Generous fieldwork expenses came on top. A norm quickly developed that entailed at least twelve months of doctoral fieldwork, often added to by a return visit during the writing-up period. Having already undertaken nine to twelve months of fieldwork for their postgraduate degree, the time spent by new PhD students in the field was altogether comparable to their British and American counterparts. Arguably, they had an advantage: they could start their PhD fieldwork with a good understanding of the socio-political situation in the selected country; they had some knowledge of the language; they had contacts. Culture shock was reduced to a minimum.

The next major upheaval came in 2003 with the Bologna agreement that introduced a radical new structure to higher education in Norway. The Bologna model, based on bachelor's, master's and doctoral degrees of three, two and three years respectively, turned out to be a challenge. While the already established PhD programme must be viewed as an improvement on the old system, the benefits of the bachelor's and master's programmes are less convincing. A three-year BA does not compare to the previous four to five years of undergraduate studies.[1] At the same time, two years of master's

---

1 At the annual conference of the Norwegian Anthropological Association in 2002, the scenarios for fieldwork in the emerging Bologna-aligned anthropology programmes in Norway were discussed in detail, which resulted in a special issue of the association's peer-reviewed journal then under my editorship, with eight original articles on fieldwork strategies in past, present and future Norwegian

studies rather than three (often four) years for the *hovedfag* meant a reduction in course work, as well as in the amount of time spent on fieldwork. And so, understandably and undeniably, the 'new' master's thesis is not of the quality we came to expect under the previous system – although there are exceptions.

Nevertheless, post-Bologna, each of Norway's four departments have given fieldwork substantial weight in their master's programmes. We still insist on five to seven months fieldwork and encourage students to travel far afield. Many do, and many write original dissertations that contribute to our knowledge of place and topic. Students get a government loan for the two years of their master's. They can apply for some extra funding (one third of which is non-repayable if the course is completed within the stipulated period) if they need to study a language *in situ*, and this we encourage. In addition, the departments offer small travel grants for those who travel outside Europe, and so money is no longer an obstacle.

Of the thirty-three master's students who graduated in 2015 at the University of Oslo, only six undertook fieldwork in Norway. While some who go abroad choose urban sites with a clear idea of what they want to study, and where English is spoken, others go for more open-ended projects in remote places. Not everyone wants to pursue an academic career, but the experience of completing fieldwork and writing a thesis on the basis of it is in itself an achievement that is intellectually stimulating, matures the mind and appears attractive to prospective employers. What we are happy to note is the enthusiastic engagement of our master's students, clearly manifest in an annual edited volume of at least ten original fieldwork-based articles by master's students at Norwegian universities, suitably entitled *Betwixt and Between*. These volumes, published continuously since 2004, demonstrate a genuine curiosity about the lives and thoughts of others, and an ability to anthropologize that curiosity in a meaningful and informed manner. While our master students are sufficiently funded to enable them to experience the challenges of serious ethnographic fieldwork, it is unfortunate that very few get the opportunity to continue to PhD level. Only those who are granted a full three-year scholarship are accepted. These PhD fellowships are few and highly competitive.

In conclusion, the Norwegian fieldwork tradition has developed along lines largely determined by external factors: degree structures, funding, opportunity – but its development has also been guided by desire. Perhaps it is not so different from that of the British?

---

anthropology. A cautious optimism was evident as departments were already shaping the new master's programmes to include a minimum of six months of fieldwork (see Howell 2002).

References

Archetti, E. 2003. *Masculinities: Football, Polo and the Tango in Argentina*. Oxford: Berg Publishers.

Archetti, E. and Stølen, K.A. 1975. *Explotación familiar y acumulación de capital en el agro argentine* [Family production and capital accumulation in the Argentinean countryside]. Buenos Aires: Siglo XXI Editores.

Barth, F. 1966. 'Models of social organization'. Occasional Paper No. 23. London: Royal Anthropological Institute.

——— 1975. *Ritual and Knowledge among the Baktaman of New Guinea*. Oslo/New Haven, CT: Universitetsforlaget/Yale University Press.

Falkenberg, A. and Falkenberg, J. 1981. *The Affinal Relationship System: A New Approach to Kinship and Marriage among the Australian Aborigines at Port Keats*. Oslo: Universitetsforlaget.

Gullestad, M. 1984. *Kitchen-Table Society: A Case Study of the Family Life and Friendships of Young Working-Class Urban Mothers in Norway*. Oslo: Universitetsforlaget.

Howell, S. 2002. 'Feltarbeid i et nytt århundre' [Fieldwork in a new century]. *Norsk Antropologisk Tidsskrift* 13:185–6.

Klausen, A.M. and Sørum, A. 1993. *Under tropenes himmel: den store norske oppdager Carl Lumholtz* [Under tropical skies: the great Norwegian explorer Carl Lumholtz]. Oslo: Tiden norsk forlag.

——— 2006. *Bajo el cielo de los trópicos: El gran explorador noruego Carl Lumholtz:100 años de testimonios de los pueblos indígenas*. Mexico: Comisión Nacional para el Desarrollo de los Pueblos Indígenas.

Lumholtz, C. 1889. *Among Cannibals: An Account of Four Years Travels in Australia and of Camp Life with the Aborigines of Queensland*. New York: Scribner.

——— 1902. *Unknown Mexico: A Record of Five Years' Exploration among the Tribes of the Western Sierra Madre; in the Tierra Caliente of Tepic and Jalisco; and among the Tarascos of Michoacan*. New York: Scribner.

Rudie, I. 1962. 'Endring i et marginalt samfunn: en økologisk analyse' [Changes in a marginal society: an ecological analysis]. *Magister Artium* thesis. Oslo: University of Oslo.

——— 1994. *Visible Women in East Coast Malay Society: On the Reproduction of Gender in Ceremonial, School and Market*. Oslo: Scandinavian University Press

Siverts, H. 1960. 'Political organization in a Tzeltal community in Chaipas, Mexico'. *Alpha Kappa Deltan* 30:14–28.

Sommerfelt, A. 1958. *Politisk kohesjon i et statsløst samfunn: Tallensiene i nordterritoriet av Gullkysten (Ghana)* [Political cohesion in a stateless society: the Tallensi of the Northern Territories of the Gold Coast (Ghana)]. Oslo: A.W. Brøggers Boktrykkeri A/S.

4

No direction home?

Anthropology in and of Norway

HALVARD VIKE

✦

On 'home blindness'

When watching Martin Scorsese's documentary about Bob Dylan, No Direction Home, one inevitably gets the impression that Dylan wants to tell us that he actually came from nowhere.[1] Hibbing, Minnesota, where Dylan grew up, is referred to only as a bleak, general kind of place in the shadow of Dylan's fame, and, according to commentator Roger Ebert, he 'mentions his father only because he bought the house where Dylan found a guitar'.[2] Thus it seems very hard to grasp where Dylan's particular view of the world came from, at least as far as what influenced him prior to his arrival in New York City.

I want to suggest that anthropologists, perhaps somewhat like Dylan, often tend to appear as people from nowhere, studying others as 'locals' – people who are socially embedded in worlds more or less radically different from that of the anthropologist. It is illustrative, therefore, that anthropologists tend to talk about doing anthropology in the country where they were themselves born and socialized as 'doing anthropology at home' (Gullestad 2001; Jackson 1987). Perhaps because they perceive of themselves as possessing an abstract form of identity, they tend to see any local spot in the country in which they grew up as a version of their 'home', or 'their own' place.

---

1   M. Scorsese (dir.), *No Direction Home: Bob Dylan*, 208 mins. Paramount Pictures, 2005.

2   R. Ebert, Review of Scorcese (dir.), *No Direction Home: Bob Dylan*. Rogerebert. com, 19 September 2005 (www.rogerebert.com/reviews/no-direction-home-bob-dylan-2005, accessed 26 September 2019).

In my understanding, this positioning is not well suited for understanding what the anthropologist really shares with those who are being studied, what they understand by studying them or what it is that may be different between the anthropologist's world and that of their interlocutors. The position in fact disposes anthropologists to claim familiarity on false premises. Claiming familiarity in this way echoes Ernest Gellner's portrait of the enlightened, European elites in the era of revolutionary nationalism: these elites insisted that every peasant was a natural emblem of the nation and gave the peasants a slot in the greater narrative of the elite's burden to represent and classify the whole (Gellner 1983). Surely, the metaphor of 'doing anthropology at home' is a bad one. That is why, I argue, anthropologists' discussions of the special pitfalls they may fall into, and the challenges these represent for the discipline, tend to miss the point. The discussions reflect, furthermore, deeper problems related to the conceptualization of culture as a holistic entity. In this context, I argue that the issue at stake is whether the relationship between the anthropologist and those studied may generate some common good, that is to say, some kind of shared interests stemming from mutual understanding. It is not enough that the anthropologist simply 'feels' that they have understood the culture of the Other.

If we try to move beyond the metaphor of 'home' and look more closely at the anthropological discourse of problematic familiarity, which is to say familiarity of the kind that supposedly makes anthropologists 'home blind', clearly the main problem is epistemological and relational, rather than a property of the object of study. Very few anthropologists have reported that they, as 'natives', automatically blended in so well with their informants that they failed to understand that they were creators of culture. On the one hand, the claim that it is unattractive, uninteresting and/or not fascinating enough to do fieldwork 'at home' is indeed quite commonly made, at least in anthropological seminars in Norway. On the other hand, the debate about the construction of otherness in anthropology is clearly linked to a certain distaste for what we construct as familiar, ordinary and perhaps socially awkward on a more personal level.

Ideas of what 'home' is and where it is located are reflected in specific anthropological constructions of culture – that is, culture as somehow linked to nation – as difference of the kind that produces culture shock and/or visible boundaries, or as an aspect of clearly delineated and homogeneous social groups, such as 'little traditions' and communities. This may in part explain why anthropologists have largely left the study of the major institutions of Western society to sociologists, economists and political scientists. Also, it brings the social status and taste of the anthropologist into the light. Fieldwork in contexts that mobilize the familiarity syndrome in the anthropologist brings them into situations where informants tend to make claims directly related to the anthropologist's social status and taste, and most probably their political interests too (Jørgensen 2017). To contain this becomes a form of anthropological self-defence.

Marilyn Strathern, in her discussion on 'auto-anthropology' (Strathern 1987), insists, if I have understood her correctly, that the salient feature of doing anthropology 'at home' is that anthropologists and those under study are somehow in the same business of creating accounts of culture and society. They share the idea that they are taking part in constructing their own world and are creating 'societies', while also sharing the sense that 'culture' is a conceptual device that denotes them both. Her concern is not so much the social relationship between these actors and the way it influences anthropological epistemology but one of overlapping genres. In the context of 'home', anthropological accounts are 'continuous with indigenous form' (ibid.:18), and the anthropological endeavour is no longer one of translating one culture into the terms of another.

Strathern's point is interesting and important because she places the issue firmly within the domain of the anthropology of knowledge construction, and she demonstrates that the idea of doing anthropology at 'home' is not primarily about how exotic the cultural attributes of those studies appear to be, but rather how they construct knowledge (ibid.:16). 'Auto-anthropology', according to Strathern, is the practice of doing fieldwork in the context of where anthropology itself was invented. However, this does not guarantee that mutual understanding will evolve (see below). In fact, a sharp discontinuity may arise precisely because the two parties produce differing narratives from (some of) the same epistemological premises. The anthropological version may be viewed as a variant of the informant's own, which the former is meant to supplant (ibid.:24).

In the following, I will look more closely at anthropological studies of Norwegian society. This exploration may prove interesting because it allows us to view Strathern's idea of 'continuity with indigenous form' from a very different perspective – not as something emanating from some essential similarity, but rather as a phenomenon emerging from a particular form of anthropological practice and construction of culture (in analytical terms).

Aspects of the ethnography of Norway

The anthropology of Norway was profoundly shaped by Fredrik Barth and his vision of social anthropology as the study of generative process. It so happened that the anthropology of Norway was elaborated in a context where the social sciences, along with the growth of academic institutions, expanded considerably and were conceptualized largely as integral parts of a general process of political mobilization. The relevant societal metaphor was not culture but rather politics – understood in Barthian terms as negotiation, choice, interest and alliance formation, and power asymmetry. Although Barth himself did not concern himself much with politics as such – even if that was a main focus of his study of political leadership in Swat (Barth 1959) and a few other works – many of his students did, attracted by the potential his anthropological toolkit provided for them in that regard. Interestingly, in contrast to other disciplines like institutional economics, political science, history and parts of sociology, anthropology in Norway did not, however, enter directly into state-building projects, but remained in part outside them, with a substantial appeal among important social movements.

Prior to Fredrik Barth's entry into the academic scene in Norway, anthropology 'at home' had started in the classical manner as a study of the primitives within. The great ancestor of Norwegian sociology, Eilert Sundt (1817–1875), conducted fieldwork among the lower classes around the mid 1800s. His work began as a search for why civilization failed to take root among the lower classes, but later it became a source for serious reflection on the relationship between social inequality and ways of life (see Sundt 2006). For a number of reasons, including perhaps the tradition Sundt initiated, modern social anthropology in Norway never developed a clear, hegemonic idea of the prototypical object of study, and thus it created a space for students with very different motivations. In fact, doing fieldwork in Norway became acceptable and commonplace, and Norwegian ethnography came to be seen as a natural part of the discipline's total repertoire.

When I entered the master's programme in social anthropology in Oslo in 1990, I got the impression that only two things were paramount: doing good fieldwork, which meant mapping social interaction ethnographically, and analysing data from a processual and comparative perspective. The discipline was expanding rapidly and student numbers exploded. There was little discussion about the boundaries of the discipline; rather, there was a strong sense of identity and even a certain eagerness to explore the territories of neighbouring disciplines. For the public, anthropology came to be seen not as the study of the Other per se, or of the little society, but as a different and largely refreshing, comparative perspective on politically relevant issues. Nevertheless, a certain scepticism towards carrying out fieldwork in Norway was cultivated among a few Norwegian anthropologists. Part of the reason was that some of my teachers tended to think that fieldwork in Norway represented an epistemological challenge of a particular kind. The argument was that it is hard to learn anything genuinely new when there is no real culture shock involved.

Nevertheless, the anthropological study of Norway evinces a relatively extensive fascination with the 'non-exotic' and the 'mainstream'. One of the principal contributors to this work has been Marianne Gullestad. In the context of this book, her identification of 'sameness' as a powerful mechanism of making equality real in social interactions is particularly significant. In Norway, she argues, it is very common to insist that meaningful interaction can only take place if those involved de-emphasize the differences between them, particularly differences pertaining to rank (Gullestad 1989:109–23). Gullestad's first major work was a study of an old, working-class neighbourhood in Norway's second largest city, Bergen (Gullestad 1979). In this and later works on related themes, she found that class was only peripherally relevant to how people with different class backgrounds identified themselves. Working-class people tended to see themselves as having the same set of values as anyone else, except snobbish people and deviant individuals.

This insight echoes Jan-Petter Blom's classic study of the mountain farmers and valley farmers of inland South Norway (Blom 1969). Although mountain farmers saw themselves as different from their more affluent valley neighbours, they largely embraced the values of these significant others and tried, if ambivalently, to adopt those values. Blom demonstrated that his case was one of inverted ethnicity. Although mountain farmers fulfilled all the basic criteria of an ethnic group vis-à-vis their valley neighbours, as anthropologists had identified these criteria in the study of symbiotic relations between the various groups of South-East Asia in particular, they still, at the same time, embraced the 'modern', bourgeois or middle-class-oriented values of the valley farmers in part because, for them, these values represented a vehicle for social mobility. Gullestad's and Blom's observations would indicate that in Norway there may be rather strong cultural currents working against cultural segmentation, despite the fact that cultural differences that could turn into ethnic ones can be found all over the place. How are we to understand this in broader analytical terms?

In several later works by Norwegian anthropologists looking at aspects of 'Norwegian culture', a key assumption is that a peasant heritage is still strong and that the normal life of a modern, class-based, capitalist society – influenced primarily by life in the metropolis – has somehow not yet found its way into the patterns of national culture. In a study of Norwegian social democracy, Tian Sørhaug (1986) touched on the problem of morality. Public morality in Norwegian society, he argues, is a product of the metaphorical power of the close-knit community where everyone knows everyone else. This inclines the population to see the national polity as consisting of people who are all essentially the same. The other side of the coin is that Norwegians, so immersed in this not-yet-fully modernized cultural system, have a hard time developing a critical, distrustful attitude towards their leaders and the institutions they run, as long as they seem to follow the rules and look okay. In small communities, everyone tends to think that all have identical interests, Sørhaug adds. In several publications, Marianne Gullestad argues in a somewhat similar vein, emphasizing that 'egalitarian individualism' has a lot to do with Norwegians' love of their home (see Gullestad 1989). Two closely related observations made by Gullestad are worth mentioning: first, that the home serves as an important metaphorical inspiration for the idea of the nation of equals; and second, that people's love of their home somehow makes them able to resist the pressures of markets and bureaucracies that dominate the public domain:

> In contemporary folk theory, the home, the family, and the intimate sphere represent a sharp contrast to larger society, particularly bureaucratic organizations. The intimate sphere constitutes a space where people feel a sense of control and where bureaucracy, according to most people, should not be allowed to expand. In a very special way, the home represents intimacy, privacy, wholeness and the personal in contrast to the bureaucratic, instrumental, efficient and specialized.
>
> (ibid.:175)

In order to establish a critical angle on the arguments put forth by Sørhaug and Gullestad, we may turn to John Barnes's work in western Norway in the 1950s (Barnes 1954). Barnes demonstrated that the egalitarian ethos and the organization of trust in close-knit informal networks were intimately related to community politics (as opposed to the home and 'traditional' arenas). Barnes identified 'committees and class'[3] as salient features of the local world he observed. He saw Bremnes and other peripheral areas of Norway as characterized by a void where the conventional state apparatus was largely absent, mainly due to the Norwegian separation from Denmark in 1814, and later from Sweden in 1905. The local political life Barnes observed was, in his understanding, gradually filling this void. Committees represented 'a common pattern of organization that occurs in every instance of formal social life' (ibid.:50), which is to say a committee for each association, elected by an annual meeting, with an executive council, a chairman, treasurer and a secretary – all based on a simple majority vote. Barnes further speculated about what type of social class system Bremnes would turn out to have in the future. He saw the social process he described as necessarily transitional, and

---

3   Barnes refers to formal political committees as well as, say, the board of a voluntary organisation.

expected increasing class differences to undermine both the role of part-time peasants and that of committees.

Social inequality was clearly present in Bremnes at the time of Barnes's fieldwork, but a strongly egalitarian code of behaviour seemed to make it largely irrelevant. Barnes assumed that this situation would change as inequality grew stronger. He observed that Bremnes's 'part-time peasants' had involved themselves in commercial fishing from very early on, in much the same way as 'peasants' in other parts of the country had done in the timber trade. At the time of his fieldwork, the fishing industry was expanding, establishing what Barnes saw as a more 'modern' system of hierarchical relations than the ones he observed in politics and social networks in the community. Although Barnes's perspective clearly differs from that of Gullestad and Sørhaug in that he acknowledges the significance of 'public culture' and the power of politics in forming identities and the social organization of society, he seemed to share their assumption that the reality he observed was somehow not fully modernized. In other words, they were 'traditional' and on the margins of something else, something more modern.

Nevertheless, Barnes's pioneering interest in political activity among 'part-time peasants' demonstrated that his informants were members of formally organized committees that overlapped with informal networks of kin, neighbours, friends and workmates. In Bremnes, the idea of egalitarianism emerged as a combination of a worldview, certain universal citizen rights, a style of interaction and – perhaps above all – an institutional mechanism for dealing with political conflict. Barnes emphasized that political conflict, when channelled through discussions in the committees and the municipal assembly, mostly ended up in unanimous votes. Although in his account the description of how this was actually done, who the actors where, whom they represented, what their aims were, how they thought about what they were doing and so on is quite thin, it remains quite fascinating.

First of all, Barnes indicates that the formal roles and relationships assumed by local actors in political activities were of primary importance. These roles and relationships did not constitute a layer on top of other identities related to kinship, neighbourhood and such, but rather, at least to a large extent, substituted them. Second, the matters they dealt with in these formal capacities were not private or quasi-private, but genuinely public ones. Third and finally, it seems that these roles and relationships contributed strongly to shaping local people's social ontology, which is to say their idea of what kinds of people lived in the Bremnes community. As they saw it, Bremnes people were overwhelmingly common folk. They knew that in the wider region there were some 'fine people', but they were found almost exclusively in Bergen, the regional centre. In addition, there existed a few families and individuals with special problems who needed some public (municipal) assistance. Local folks all seemed to be aware of the fact that people were not equal, literally speaking, but in politics and associational life at large, they treated each other as though they were. One person, one vote.

Public and political anthropology in Norway

As is the case in the other Nordic countries and Germany, modern anthropology in Norway relates to ethnology and folklore studies, leaving the discipline with some potentially problematic ties. However, Fredrik Barth's great influence from the early 1950s onwards gave anthropology a much more distinct identity as a social science of the new kind. Clearly, in order to reinforce that identity, Barth defined anthropology as something that stood in opposition to neighbouring disciplines, the human sciences in particular. Anthropology became a fieldwork-based, comparative and cross-cultural study of social processes from a synchronic perspective – as opposed to a study of the cultural past of 'a people'. This had some great advantages, some of which Barth himself may have never intended. As a social science proper, anthropology was able to tap into the great prestige and influence that sociology and political science had already acquired among the Norwegian public, partly as a result of economic science's great breakthrough in political planning from the 1930s onward. In the 1950s and 1960s in Norway, social science was institutionalized in highly autonomous academic institutions, and most social scientists seemed to share a strong motivation to use their autonomy to influence government policy and involve themselves in public debate. The first anthropological manifestation of this tendency was Fredrik Barth's project to take a closer look at entrepreneurship in northern Norway, which brought anthropologists into close contact with the large-scale governmental attempt to engineer social change. In his introduction to the work that emerged from that project, Barth stated that 'very frequently entrepreneurship involves the relationship between persons and institutions of one society with those of another, economically more advanced, one, and the entrepreneur becomes an essential "broker" in this situation of culture contact' (Barth 1972:5).

Shortly afterwards, one of Barth's students and a contributor to the project, Ottar Brox, wrote a book about the situation in northern Norway (Brox 1966). His book was aimed at the general public and had a very clear political message. Brox was inspired by dependency theory and brought it to bear directly on the issue of 'culture contact'. Arguing that the traditional adaptation along the coast of northern Norway – among fishermen/farmers, or 'part-time peasants', as Barnes called them – was highly rational and efficient, and both economically and ecologically highly viable, Brox demonstrated that the government's plan to modernize the region by means of massive industrialization would have far-reaching, unintended consequences. Brox hit a nerve in Norwegian society. The book became a key reference for the growing anti-urban, anti-authoritarian, environmentalist-leftist movement in the 1960s and 1970s, which culminated in the 'no' vote in Norway's referendum on joining the then European Economic Community in 1972. The electoral landslide that followed immediately after brought Brox himself a seat in parliament. Through this book, and many other later works, Brox demonstrated anthropology's relevance for understanding contemporary politics in a novel way. He showed how ethnography could strengthen our understanding of political institutions, how institutions generate worldviews (or political ideology) and how the analysis of people's lives in contemporary Norwegian society could be understood in the context of political economy.

In my own work, Brox is a major inspiration, and I will briefly emphasize one such line of inspiration that I think is worth highlighting. In my introduction to this chapter, I discussed the phenomenon of 'home blindness' and argued that Norwegian anthropology and the anthropology of Norway have never primarily been about identifying the exotics within. Some of Fredrik Barth's students realized that Barth's analytical emphasis on social process and on the need to identify generating mechanisms that could explain emerging phenomena, perhaps best illustrated in the title of his study of the Baktaman on New Guinea, *Cosmologies in the Making* (Barth 1987), could be useful for analysing political change. One such student – Brox – was himself politically very active and saw that Barth's analytical framework could be used both academically and practically. When he realized that bureaucrats and policymakers were hesitant to embrace his message, in his study of northern Norway he went on to explore anthropologically why this was the case. This was part of a much larger project: to try to understand why state authorities failed (or were simply unwilling) to grasp the idea that their grandiose plans of transforming northern Norway into a series of industrial centres did not at all appeal to the coastal population, who utilized the resources available to them in ways that seemed both meaningful, efficient and sustainable – largely by combining fishing, small-scale agriculture and seasonal wage labour. One important aspect of his research agenda emerging from this was an ambition to explain how political and bureaucratic institutions conceptualize, represent and act on the interests of those whom they are supposed to represent. He developed an acute sensibility to unintended consequences, and his analytical programme became largely one of explaining how the mechanisms generating undesirable policy outcomes actually worked, as well as how ideological ideas and programmes (and more mundane things, such as self-interest) prevented them from being acknowledged and dealt with (see Brox 2016). As noted above, Brox's work is distinctly 'Barthian'. However, even though Brox has had a profound influence on political mobilization in Norway, most clearly expressed in the EEC and EU referendums in 1972 and 1994 (both resulting in a majority vote against membership), his anthropological impact outside Scandinavia has been limited.

As with many other students attracted to Barth's intellectual depth and charisma, Ottar Brox cared little for cultural history. The emphasis was on the here and now. The confidence in the synchronic perspective was so great that anthropologists could use it to write the history of the future, as in Brox's case, and reconstruct the past in terms of the present, as Barth had tried to do in his work on Swat Pathans (Barth 1959). Perhaps more importantly, Brox did not seem to care much about the fact that northern Norway was 'home' for him. Although his work was in part inspired by Barth's idea of the entrepreneurial domain as an interface between cultures, he, like his teacher, was mostly concerned with institutions and micro-contexts, not cultures. In fact, the same can be said of many other Norwegian anthropologists of Brox's generation, especially those whose work included a feminist dimension (e.g. Holtedahl 1986; Rudie 1984). The study of households as a microcosm of social change caught the attention of many and had far-reaching implications for the anthropology of Norway and beyond. What these anthropologists did, among other things, was to develop models for understanding the institutionalization of the social democratic state at the local level. A key figure here was Marianne Gullestad. As indicated above, through a long series of contributions, Gullestad took the household orientation many steps further and opened up several analytical paths that have been extremely influential among colleagues and students ever since. Gullestad's originality lies in part in her ability to analyse these phenomena as a part of the everyday life of members of the majority culture without, however, ever making culture into some bounded whole. Her theory of the Nordic version of 'egalitarian individualism' is a relevant case in point. According to Gullestad, 'egalitarian individualism' is to be seen as an interactional style, or code of behaviour, and is about the pragmatic agreement between social actors and how, in order to relate meaningfully to each other, the relations must rest on the mutual acknowledgement of 'sameness' (see Gullestad 1989).

It should be pointed out here that, unlike Barth, Brox, Gullestad and their followers, Barnes did in fact care about history. In an attempt to contextualize his analysis of Bremnes as a highly egalitarian community, he noted that Norway did not really have a state until quite recently. The end of Danish colonial rule created a vacuum in rural areas that brought 'part-time peasants into key positions in the structure of government and organized social life' (Barnes 1954:57). Barnes's underlying assumption that modernization had taken place at a relatively late stage because of the postcolonial vacuum has, as shown above, surfaced in many later anthropological studies of Norway. Surely, it has stimulated the idea that after all there is something exotic to be found here. Yet Barnes's most important contribution (besides inventing 'network' as an analytical concept) has never seemed to have been systematically followed up in anthropological studies of Scandinavia: his fascinating ethnographic mapping of how patterns of interaction and power were intimately linked with the ways in which people moved in and out of institutions. Gullestad became mainly concerned with everyday life in private and informal contexts and later with public discourse, and Barth's and Brox's early interest in such matters were never really linked to Barnes's nor followed up by others in any systematic manner.

As far as I can see, the most important question in Barnes's study with direct relevance to cultural history is what it meant for people in Bremnes to be members of what he called 'committees'. In order to understand this, it is important to bear in mind that the committees he studied constituted the backbone of institutionalized municipal politics. At the same time, they were a part of a wider system of overlapping memberships in a variety of formally organized institutions that served the collective interest. In comparative terms, this is significant mainly because of the political and economic interests that gave rise to such institutions – voluntary organizations, as they are called in the civil society genre – which were of fundamental interest to most people in Bremnes and were definitely not simply created in a power vacuum nor introduced by the modernizing Norwegian state. In fact, the coastal regions of Norway, as well as inland areas from which timber could be transported along waterways, were among the most expansive pre-industrial economies in Europe. Even more importantly, there were few possibilities for monopolizing fish and timber and the channels of value that they opened up (Dyrvik 1979). And because the labour necessary to extract these sources of value was scarce, labour was organized in much the same way as were traditional work parties among peasants and in the organized resistance against representatives of the Danish state. It is not a wild generalization to state that in economic and political terms, Scandinavia was 'modernized' very early on and in somewhat different terms than many other areas of Europe (ibid.). Capitalist expansion was indeed thorough, but it took a much more local form than in most of the rest of Europe and was much less monopolist. As the old elites were never really capable of crushing or pacifying popular movements as they became politicized, only of curbing them somewhat, these movements may represent a deeper continuity in Scandinavia (where they were able to influence the state for a very long period) than in most other parts of Europe, where the state has been much more successful in reproducing pre-industrial forms of authority and hierarchy (Knudsen and Rothstein 1994).

Being a member of a voluntary organization seems to be strongly associated with a specific form of morality. The Finnish historian Henrik Stenius (1997) clearly grasped this phenomenon. In his terms, a key emergent property of voluntary associations that manage collective interests is conformity. According to Stenius, this particular way of managing collective goods – that is, through the horizontal solidarity of membership rather than hierarchical command and personal dependency – stimulates informal control of a kind that often tends to be reinforced by formal membership. This is Gullestad's egalitarian individualism revisited, but with a different source than informal, everyday life. In voluntary organizations of this type, politics is everywhere at all times. Mutual social control often seems to include all or most aspects of life because the management of the common good depends on trust, and trust in turn tends to rest on rich information concerning people's behaviour.

This may be why the preference for organized social relations of all kinds has been so strong in the Nordic region; it allows for control over collectively controlled resources and provides people with the possibility of keeping their distance from each other – a formula that, in part, sums up a Nordic version of individual autonomy. Stenius's main point, however, is that in the Nordic countries this morality was generalized, heavily influencing not only social relations in local communities but also the public sphere and, to some extent, even the state. A very good illustration here is the temperance movement in the early nineteenth century (Stenius 2010). The movement, especially in Sweden and Norway, grew out of local concerns, but very soon it gained significant national influence. Simply speaking, its goal was to make the transition from work to home as short as possible for working-class men, thereby inspiring a certain distaste for places where they could congregate without some useful common purpose. Its agenda – a very restrictive, and partly aggressive (or perhaps we should say generous) preventive alcohol policy – was translated into national policy quickly and without much hesitation. In comparative terms, it is quite remarkable that it has not, as of yet, stimulated general opposition against the state's right to invade civil society and private lives. The state has not, until quite recently at least, been perceived primarily as something one needs to avoid and seek protection from, but rather as an essential part of everyone's environment (Trägårdh 2007). As I have indicated above, the historical roots of this mindset go way back. The Scandinavian states appear, to many observers, as somewhat peculiar, and often as quite interesting – apparently due to the mysterious combination of humanism and bureaucratic standardization (Zetterberg 1986). In Scandinavia, both the belief that the state can be used to solve major collective problems and that its bureaucracy can be freedom-generating rather than humiliating is still quite robust. How do we explain this?

Hans Magnus Enzensberger, who made a journalistic tour of Sweden and Norway in the 1980s and wrote a book on each country, went to great pains to find out more about this. His attempt seems illustrative of a general trend: he suggested that people's acceptance of the intervening state in all aspects of life is somehow a product of a lack of experience (or modernization). In his account of Sweden, Enzensberger writes:

> Swedish citizens are always willing to comply with their authorities with
> such naiveté and trust as if the benevolence of the authorities were beyond
> question ... No doubt this blissful credulity has many causes. The most
> important of these is probably a lack of experience, for which one can
> only envy the Swedes. Political powers in this country have since time
> immemorial refrained from a pastime that has been daily fare in other parts
> of the world: armed persecution of citizens.
>
> (quoted in Zetterberg 1986:92)

As a result, Enzensberger adds, the institutions of the welfare state can be characterized by a 'kind of moral immunity' and are thus able to penetrate 'all crevices of daily life' while they regulate 'the affairs of individuals to an extent that is without comparison in free societies' (quoted in Zetterberg 1986:93). It may not appear strange or surprising that many commentators – such as journalists, anthropologists, sociologists – share Enzensberger's fascination with this phenomenon, but the fact that very few of them have tried seriously to understand it by actually studying it and – only then – to try to explain it, for example in line with the approach developed by John Barnes, does demand attention. As I have indicated above, Enzensberger's idea of 'moral immunity' seems deeply misplaced in light of the fact that the participatory culture inspired by Scandinavian social movements penetrated state institutions quite deeply, particularly at the local level. One essential aspect of the political economy of membership, based on the widespread idea that membership is a general metaphor for citizenship in Scandinavia, is egalitarian social control (Vike 1997). In voluntary associations, which have been highly influential in Scandinavia and contributed heavily to forming public institutions as well as the very idea of 'the state' (Vike 2013, 2017), the common good is normally carefully guarded by members who actively try to prevent elected representatives from gaining autonomy and to ensure that they stick to their mandate as it is defined by the collective. The institutions of the welfare state were never uprooted from local networks organized by membership, and the autonomy of public institutions is only partial. In my own research on local politics and bureaucracy, I have tried to illuminate and explain why not even the managerial revolution introduced by New Public Management, nor the more encompassing waves of neoliberalism since the 1980s, have successfully transformed this pattern (Bendixsen *et al.* 2018; Vike 2017). One major reason for this seems to be that the institutional structure of the Norwegian state has been unusually dispersed and heavily moored in municipalities, the autonomy of which has proven hard to undermine due to local resistance.

Conclusions

Despite the problematic colonial discourse of the savage slot in anthropology, our (we, anthropologists) devotion to difference is not primarily about the exotic Other, but about mapping variation and thinking comparatively – as well as being involved with dealing with the concept of culture as made up of forms of knowledge that people use to make sense of social interaction and attribute meaning. However, the tendency to apply the idea of the encounter of the anthropological self with the distant, subordinated, colonial other as a general model of ethnographic study seems to have inspired the attribution of inherent exoticism to the object of ethnographic study. As a result, almost by default most other ethnographic settings were perceived as out of place because they appeared closer – and often too close – to 'home'. As I have tried to argue in this chapter, the idea of 'home' in anthropology may be understood in terms of anthropological theories of the nation: an 'imagined community' projected by a self in a very specific historical and existential position. And, as was the case with national elites in the era of nation-building in the nineteenth century in particular (and which is still the case in some places), academic elites claiming ownership to the concept of culture tend to claim the 'homeness' of the entire imagined community.

The anthropology of Norway is interesting in this regard because in its early phase it became characterized by a certain ignorance concerning anthropology's colonial heritage. Emerging from this situation was a certain epistemological naiveté – the self/other problem was hardly discussed until the 1980s – but at the same time a possibility for a kind of fresh start emerging from the Barthian revolution of the 1950s. The pioneering, and very pragmatic, activities of Fredrik Barth during the initial phase of anthropology in Norway from the late 1950s onwards inspired students not only to leave for fieldwork in faraway places, but also, often in addition to and in between these endeavours, to explore a variety of social contexts in Norway ethnographically. With his relatively privileged background and scholarly ideas of scientific autonomy, Barth himself did not identify strongly with oppositional social movements and was not very interested in making anthropology politically relevant. However, he was extremely efficient in relating to the public's rising fascination in anthropology and in utilizing this as a means for institutional support and disciplinary expansion. In this process, Barth became a renowned enlightenment figure in Norway. He established close links between being a public intellectual and being expected to invest one's expertise in some 'useful' way, which is to say to contribute optimistically to social reform.

There is no doubt that many of Barth's students were inspired by this way of doing things, but most probably their sense of facing the unique possibility brought by anthropology – to bring social science into closer contact with the concerns of the people they studied – emerged in more indirect ways. Many of these students came from humble backgrounds and had very strong ties to the social movements in which the new generation of 'politically conscious' academics were expected to take part. Partly for this reason, there seems to have existed a sense among the first generation of anthropologists (after Barth) that the Other was not simply an object of study, and certainly not someone who primarily belonged to 'a culture', but rather – sometimes directly, but most often indirectly, I suppose – someone who already included an agenda that held a possible contribution to anthropology. A characteristic feature of the type of anthropological practice developed by Fredrik Barth's students was the adaptation of ethnographically derived analytical models to projects already defined by the people under study: models that, in turn, helped redefine and sharpen these projects.

A characteristic feature of the generation following Barth's anthropology was that a significant number of them became publicly relevant intellectuals *qua* their extended ethnographic involvement. Their approaches spoke to larger issues to which both 'informants' and the larger public could often both relate through politically informed agency. As a side effect of this type of ethnographic practice, anthropology was also brought closer to – and sometimes directly into – the major institutions in the market and the state. This helped undermine the widespread idea that anthropology is mostly about those things outside of formal institutions. Regardless of how interested anthropologists and others may be in Scandinavia as an ethnographic region, the anthropology of Norway (as well as of Sweden and Denmark, which I have not had the possibility to discuss here) may have something of comparative value. The conditions under which the discipline grew and thrived were quite peculiar, and interesting opportunities were explored without much concern for whether or not people, institutions and relations of power appeared sufficiently exotic.

The anthropology of Scandinavia, and Norway more specifically, was never a major or dominant element in anthropological departments in Norway, but it was emphasized quite consistently as an important element in the overall ambition to work comparatively. Today it is clear that this tradition, and the tendency to highlight public anthropology as an integral aspect of this, is less strong. I see no reason, however, to assume that it cannot be reproduced, although the political economy of anthropological career development points in other directions. For example, anthropological departments in Norway increasingly cultivate a 'publish in English only' policy, leaving communication with the public and social movements more or less secondary. Yet my impression is that the tradition I have described has left an imprint, and there are signs that it may be lasting. A significant number of academic anthropologists not only take part in public debate (for instance after returning from fieldwork elsewhere), but also involve themselves in research projects in Norway and bring their insight to bear on public debate – characteristically communicating a relativizing, comparative 'outsider gaze' in combination with engaged suggestions as to how to improve policy.

References

Barnes, J.A. 1954. 'Class and committees in a Norwegian island parish'. *Human Relations* 7(1):39–58.

Barth, F. 1959. *Political Leadership among Swat Pathans*. London: Athlone Press.

———1972 [1963]. 'Introduction'. In F. Barth (ed.), *The Role of the Entrepreneur in Social Change in Northern Norway*, pp. 5–19. Oslo: Universitetsforlaget.

——— 1987. *Cosmologies in the Making: A Generative Approach to Cultural Variation in Inner New Guinea*. Cambridge: Cambridge University Press.

Bendixsen, S., Bringslid, M. and Vike, H. (eds). 2018. *Egalitarianism in Scandinavia: Historical and Contemporary Perspectives*. New York: Palgrave MacMillan.

Blom, J.-P. 1969. 'Ethnic and cultural differentiation'. In F. Barth (ed.), *Ethnic Groups and Boundaries: The Social Organization of Culture Difference*, pp. 75–85. Oslo: Universitetsforlaget.

Brox, O. 1966. *Hva Skjer i Nord-Norge? En Studie i Norsk Utkantpolitikk* [What is happening in northern Norway? A study of Norwegian policy for marginal areas]. Oslo: Pax.

——— 2016. *På vei mot et postindustrielt klassesamfunn?* [Towards a post-industrial class society?]. Oslo: Pax.

Dyrvik, S. 1979. *Norsk økonomisk historie 1500–1970* [Norwegian economic history 1500–1970]. Bergen: Universitetsforlaget.

Gellner, E. 1983. *Nations and Nationalism*. Ithaca, NY: Cornell University Press.

Gullestad, M. 1979. *Livet i en gammel bydel: Livsmiljø og bykultur på Verftet og en del av Nøstet* [Life in an old neighbourhood: everyday life and urban culture in Verftet and part of Nøstet]. Oslo: Aschehoug.

——— 1989. *Kultur og Hverdagsliv* [Culture and everyday life]. Oslo: Universitetsforlaget.

——— 2001. 'Likhetens grenser' [The limits of equality]. In M.E Lien, H. Lidén and
      H. Vike (eds), *Likhetens Paradokser: Antropologiske Undersøkelser i det
      Moderne Norge* [Paradoxes of equality: anthropological investigations in
      modern Norway], pp. 32–67. Oslo: Universitetsforlaget.

Holtedahl, L. 1986. *Hva Mutter Gjør er Alltid Viktig: Om å Være Kvinne og Mann i
      en Nordnorsk Bygd i 1970-årene* [What Mum does is always important: on
      being woman and man in a north Norwegian parish in the 1970s]. Oslo:
      Universitetsforlaget.

Jackson, A. (ed.). 1987. *Anthropology at Home*. London: Tavistock Publications.

Jørgensen, R.E. 2017. '"Vi er altid faldet mellem flere stole": Socialøkonomi og social
      virksomhed "betwixt and between"' ['We have always fallen between two
      chairs': socio-econoomics and social work 'betwixt and between']. PhD
      thesis. Roskilde: Doctoral School of People and Technology.

Knudsen, T. and Rothstein, B. 1994. 'State building in Scandinavia'. *Comparative
      Politics* 26(2):203–20.

Rudie, I. (ed.) 1984. *Myk start – hard landing: Om forvaltning av kjønnsidentitet i en
      endringsprosess* [Soft start – hard landing: on managing gender identity in a
      process of change]. Oslo: Universitetsforlaget.

Sørhaug, H.C. 1986. 'Totemisme på norsk: betraktninger om det norske
      sosialdemokratiets vesen' [Totemism, Norwegian style: reflections on the
      nature of Norwegian social democracy]. In A.M. Klausen (ed.), *Den norske
      væremåten* [*Being Norwegian*] pp. 61–88. Oslo: Da Capo.

Stenius, H. 1997. 'The good life is a life in conformity. the impact of Lutheran
      tradition on Nordic political culture'. In Ø. Sørensen and B. Stråth (eds),
      The Cultural Construction of Norden, pp. 161–71. Oslo: Scandinavian
      University Press.

——— 2010. 'Nordic associational life in a European and an inter-Nordic perspective'.
      In H. Stenius and R. Alapuro (eds), *Nordic Associations in a European
      Perspective*, pp. 29–86. Baden-Baden: Nomos.

Strathern, M. 1987. 'The limits of auto-anthropology'. In A. Jackson (ed.),
      Anthropology at Home, pp. 16–37. London: Tavistock Publications.

Sundt, E. 2006 [1857]. *Om sædeligheds-tilstanden i Norge* [On Morality in Norway].
      Oslo: Bokklubben.

Trägårdh, L. 2007. 'The "civil society" debate in Sweden: the welfare state challenged'.
      In L. Trägårdh (ed.), *State and Civil Society in Northern Europe: The
      Swedish Model Reconsidered*, pp. 9–37. Oxford: Berghahn Books.

Vike, H. 1997. 'Reform and resistance: a Norwegian illustration'. In C. Shore and S.
      Wright (eds), *Anthropology of Policy: Critical Perspectives on Governance
      and Power*, pp. 150–65. London: Routledge.

——— 2013. 'Utopian time and contemporary time: temporal dimensions of planning and reform in the Norwegian welfare state'. In S. Abram and G. Weszkalnys (eds), *Elusive Promises: Planning in the Contemporary World*, pp. 35–57. Oxford: Berghahn Books.

——— 2017. *Politics and Bureaucracy in the Norwegian Welfare State: An Anthropological Approach*. New York: Palgrave Macmillan.

Zetterberg, H.L. 1986. 'The rational humanitarians'. In S.R. Graubard (ed.), *Norden: The Passion for Equality*, pp. 79–97. Oslo: Norwegian University Press.

5

Norwegian anthropology and development

New roles for a troubled future?

GUNNAR M. SØRBØ

❖

Two narratives

As with most other stories, the story of the relationship between Norwegian anthropology and development efforts may be told in different ways. One narrative deals with anthropology's struggle to be heard and used, as indicated by the title of an article by a historian about the relationship between Norwegian anthropologists and the Norwegian aid administration up until 1987 (Kjerland 1999). It tells about the uneasy relationship between aid and anthropology, in many ways about anthropologists' marginality. When the Norwegian government embarked on its first aid project in 1952 through a fisheries project in Kerala, India, Fredrik Barth, who was twenty-five years of age at the time, offered his services, along with Professor Gutorm Gjessing from the Ethnographic Museum of the University of Oslo. They were both turned down, but Barth was offered a clerical position where he could 'collect anthropological material in the evenings and week-ends' (ibid.:322). He declined.

For many years to come, this experience was regarded as indicative of the official attitude to anthropology. On the officials' side, anthropologists came to be 'among the most critical of Norwegian development policy and the implementation of projects' (Howell 2010:270). In Oslo, Arne Martin Klausen published a report and later wrote and published his doctoral dissertation on the Kerala project (Klausen 1968). As the senior anthropology professor in Oslo, he remained a critic of Norwegian aid, and the gist of his criticism (and that of several colleagues) was that proper account was not taken of local and social institutions and cultural values.

In Bergen, Fredrik Barth also wrote and spoke about how societies must be understood in their own terms (Barth 1968, 1972). In his intellectual biography of Barth, Thomas Hylland Eriksen writes that during the 1960s and 1970s the Bergen anthropologists were not necessarily concerned with trying to make the world a better place to live (Eriksen 2015:127). However, Barth saw applied anthropology as 'Immensely stimulating and challenging', and that it would also reveal, as he wrote, that our scholarship may often be 'incomplete and unworkable' (Barth 1981:10).

Barth never worked for the Norwegian Agency for Development Cooperation (Norad), but the United Nations Educational, Scientific and Cultural Organization (Unesco) and the Food and Agricultural Organization of the United Nations (FAO) were among his first employers (in Iran and Sudan), and he ended his career by consulting for the United Nations Children's Fund (Unicef) in Bhutan and the World Bank in China. In fact, his excellent monograph on the Basseri nomads of southern Iran (Barth 1964) and his most quoted publication on ethnicity (Barth 1969) came out of his engagement in applied anthropology, the former directly and the latter indirectly. In Iran, he was asked by Unesco to give advice on how to settle nomads. He ended up writing a report advising very much against it, praising the freedom and living conditions of the Basseri, which he deemed superior to that of most settled people in the adjoining rural areas.

In 1963/4, he served as Unesco Professor in Social Anthropology at the University of Khartoum, Sudan, then one of the best universities in sub-Saharan Africa. During his stay there, he was asked by the FAO to make an inventory and analysis of human resources in the Jebel Marra region of Darfur as a basis for formulating a development plan. Darfur was then a rather unknown place, and it was only much later (in 2003/4) that it came to international attention because of an enormous humanitarian crisis, serious conflicts, accusations of genocide and the subsequent indictment of Sudan's president, Omar el-Bashir, by the International Criminal Court. Out of this work, focused on livelihoods, came a report submitted to the FAO (Barth 1967a) and a much-quoted paper on spheres of exchange (Barth 1967b).

Barth employed Gunnar Haaland as his research assistant in Darfur. Haaland's research involved studies of Fur sedentary farmers, as well as Baggara Arabs, cattle-herders who migrated into the area in the dry season after the Fur had harvested their fields. He discovered that livestock was an attractive investment, and that some Fur farmers built up sizeable herds of cattle, established themselves as nomads and migrated with the Baggara in the rainy season. These nomadized Fur then became assimilated into Baggara groups and adopted features of Baggara culture. Ethnically, many Fur households thus became Baggara.

Out of this research came another much-quoted paper by Haaland about economic dimensions of ethnic processes (Haaland 1969), published in a book that was to a large extent inspired by Haaland's material (Eriksen 2015:104). That book, *Ethnic Groups and Boundaries*, edited by Barth (1969), has become one of the most-quoted works in anthropology. Darfur, meanwhile, became something of a textbook case for identity change (de Waal 2005:194).

These types of engagements gave rise to a second narrative about the relationship between aid and academia, which was less concerned with anthropology's struggle to be heard and used, and more about the methodological and other challenges involved in applying anthropology to practical problems.

The applicability of anthropology

When I joined the Bergen anthropology department as a student in 1968, there were frequent discussions of policy and practice. The presence of Ottar Brox as a research fellow was particularly significant in this regard. Brox had his basic training in rural sociology, and was already famous for his book (in Norwegian) on northern Norway (Brox 1966). He was a prolific writer on many different, mostly Norwegian, political issues, and, while not being an anthropologist himself, he later wrote that his analytical tool box came from anthropology as it was practised and taught during the 1960s in Bergen (Brox 2013:93). In a book he published on 'practical social science', also in Norwegian, there are seven references to Fredrik Barth's works (Brox 1991).

This was the age of mimeographed typescripts, papers that had been mostly handwritten, given to a secretary to type, presented at conferences or seminars, circulated among colleagues but remaining unpublished, with authors receiving other typescripts from friends and colleagues in return. In Oslo, there was a well-known mimeo by Jorun Solheim that was critical of Barth's writings – about Barth and Bailey standing on the shoulders of Radcliffe-Brown and Firth (Solheim 1975). In Bergen, there was a paper by Brox (in Norwegian) on 'generative planning' (Brox 1971) and a paper by Barth (originally given as a lecture given at a UNESCO seminar) that was influential (particularly among students), despite its rather boring title: 'Sociological aspects of integrated surveys for river basin development' (Barth 1970). Some of us still have copies, now yellowish with age.

Barth and Brox held similar views on the requirement that social science be applicable (not necessarily applied, which may only happen rarely). It must be decision-oriented and explain conditions in society with the help of categories that contain possibilities for action. If, for example, anthropologists are asked by the county of Finnmark in the far north of Norway to find out how they can reduce the number of young people who migrate southwards, anthropologists have to search for variables that the authorities could do something about and influence. Anthropologists may, of course, find that there is not much that can be done locally about such out-migration – for example, that those with the best grades in school leave Finnmark for better pastures further south – but that is an empirical question (Brox 2013).

This means that in order for social science to be applicable, its practitioners have to construct models with which they can try to trace the unintended consequences of alternative interventions and make explicit statements on the interrelationships between interventions on the one hand and the decisions and behaviour of identified actors on the other. This calls for conceptual models that allow for the formulation of conditional hypotheses – that is, we need models that allow us to deduce what behavioural responses are likely to follow from specific empirical conditions. As Barth wrote, the more the anthropologist's methodology takes the form of simulation models, the more adequate the analysis will be (Barth 1970).

Barth also wrote that it is unrealistic to hope that we can build an analytical model that includes all the relevant factors and provides a firm basis for the evaluation of alternative interventions: 'We must be satisfied with something much more pragmatic: the accumulation of data that provide a basis for improvement and correction of policy' (ibid.). One of anthropology's main contributions is to limit the margin of error in project formulation, to state what cannot or should not be done (see also Haaland 1982). In the same vein, Brox quoted Karl Popper (1969) as saying that we are not able to construct happiness, but we can easily recognize and identify the opposite (misery or unhappiness), which should be reduced or preferably eliminated. Only by analysing how the undesired or dysfunctional features of society are generated can we help to reduce or remove them (Brox 2013:91–2).

Most of Barth's own experience of policy and practice was based on his work for UN organizations, but in the early 1970s, he managed to convince Norad (which was then headed by a former admiral) to employ Georg Henriksen from the Bergen department to do research among Turkana pastoralists in northern Kenya, who were subject to massive Norwegian aid efforts, including attempts to make them into fishermen. While Norad did not like what he wrote about the failure to build development efforts on existing human resources (Henriksen 1974), several colleagues in the following years received modest funds from Norad's research office (including students going to Sudan and Kenya) or were hired as consultants in different countries, both for baseline studies and project monitoring.

From about the mid 1970s until the late 1980s, there was a rising demand for anthropologists, mainly due to a new development discourse that included an emphasis on popular participation and empowerment, integrated rural development programmes and the idea that 'small is beautiful'. This shift provided opportunities for anthropologists as well as NGOs.

The Bergen-based Chr. Michelsen Institute (CMI), which had established a development research programme in 1965 based on a grant from the Rockefeller Foundation and with close ties to Harvard University, hired its first anthropologist and non-economist (Gunnar Haaland) in 1981 (today, the anthropology group at CMI is currently the largest in Norway outside universities). The University of Bergen established a Centre for Development Studies (CDS) in 1986, and most of its research staff were anthropologists. During this period, several Norwegian anthropologists from both Oslo and Bergen (Marit Melhuus, Kristi Anne Stølen, Tone Bleie, Karin Ask) were also at the forefront when it came to promoting the role of women in development. This resulted in Norad drafting an action plan and funding a special research programme on 'women and development' through the Research Council of Norway.

The Sudan engagement: new and enduring challenges

Barth's visiting professorship at the University of Khartoum and his consultancy work in Darfur, at a time when there was no official Norwegian interest in Sudan, initiated a history of more than fifty years of active collaboration between Bergen and Khartoum. It has included the implementation of several research programmes, competence building, student exchanges and different types of applied or policy-oriented engagements. In one case, the engagement in fact went beyond the expected limits, as one of our Sudanese colleagues (with a doctorate in anthropology from Bergen) chose to leave academia to join the rebellion in Darfur against the central government. In another case, one of our Sudanese students ended up writing a doctoral thesis at the University of Sussex, which, it has been claimed, was the main source of inspiration for a secretly circulated 'black book' documenting power relations and gross inequalities in Sudan (Abbaker 1985; Takana 2016:25).

According to Norwegian diplomats, if it had not been for these long-term efforts in research, it is unlikely that Norway would have engaged – as part of a troika with the United States and the United Kingdom – in trying to build peace in Sudan. The first Norwegian peace initiative was the Bergen Peace Forum in 1989, initiated by one Sudanese and one Norwegian anthropologist just a few months before Islamic fundamentalists came to power through a coup (Ahmed and Sørbø 1989). In 2019, after thirty years in power, they were finally toppled by a people's revolution.

The engagement in Sudan plays a major role in the history of anthropology in Bergen. It provides an example of a more or less continuous interplay between basic and applied, policy-oriented research, of genuine research cooperation with Sudanese colleagues and universities, and of the need for anthropological research to respond to new challenges, both political and theoretical (Sørbø 2016). Under the aegis of the Khartoum–Bergen relationship, anthropological research came to both complement and add to the work carried out by Barth and Haaland in the 1960s. A continued concern with changing livelihoods, mostly in the peripheries of an increasingly polarized and violent country, came to direct much of the research towards understanding underlying patterns of conflict in Sudanese society.

In the 1970s and 1980s, because of drought and famine, there was a fear that large parts of Sudan's savannah region were subject to ecological deterioration, even desertification, and that this would lead to an increase in resource-based conflicts. However, most of the research revealed that several instances of 'resource conflict' were not based on resource scarcity as such and did not necessarily lead to degradation; rather, they were political in nature and required a larger scope of investigation (Manger 2002). Conflicts increasingly erupted over access to land, and in several places they were made worse by land dispossession instigated by successive governments as part of their drive to modernize agriculture. This led to poverty, displacement of large populations and reduced pasture areas for pastoralists, but also to political mobilization and serious conflict; and once conflicts erupted, they tended to be interpreted in tribal and ethnic terms, and were often linked to other types of conflicts, leading to their escalation.

While Barth and Haaland had paid scant attention to macro-level processes, more attention had to be given to the nature of the larger social orders that impact on local communities and livelihood groups and those in which ethnic identities operate. Increasingly, it was recognized that the wars and conflicts that had spread throughout many parts of Sudan since the 1980s were part of a pattern of violence in which the Sudanese state – as a vehicle for special-interest groups – played a major role (Sørbø and Ahmed 2013).

Dealing with issues of scale, or micro–macro relations, became a key aspect of the research on Sudan. It became important to analyse regions as ongoing concerns of interdependent activities; to investigate how local conflicts were increasingly absorbed into, enmeshed with or affected by macro-political conflicts and operated in a feedback loop with them; how the multiple involvements of the international community affected local life in places like Darfur, for example, by taking issues of justice out of local hands and transferring them to the International Criminal Court in the Hague; or how the simplistic international discourse on Darfur has led to the demonization of Arab groups, even those who have tried to stay clear of violence.

Another Barthian initiative, starting with a Burg Wartenstein (Austria) symposium on issues of scale and social organization (Barth 1978) came to inspire much of the research in Sudan. This applies also to the work done by Reidar Grønhaug in Turkey and Afghanistan (e.g. Grønhaug 1978). The point is that events and developments in Darfur, like elsewhere in Sudan, must be understood in the context of a number of factors at different levels of scale. Our challenge has become that of integrating different levels of analysis, and one way of approaching this is to define the different (micro and macro) contexts that are relevant for understanding real life processes at local levels. This raises the issue of how we most fruitfully define and delimit social, economic and political systems in different local settings. The scale at which an analysis is pitched will tend to affect the types of explanations given. There is clearly no 'correct' scale for an investigation of, say, conflicts in Darfur, but there may be an appropriate one for answering different questions (Sørbø 2003).

The need to construct chains of causation through what Andrew Vayda (1983) calls 'progressive contextualization' in order to make our models 'workable' became particularly crucial in applied research assignments. Thus, if farmers on the large agricultural schemes in Sudan invest in livestock because the income derived from irrigated agriculture is insufficient, and if in so doing they contribute towards overgrazing, it is unrealistic to combat ecological deterioration by looking for management solutions for the grazing areas alone. While our instinct and training as anthropologists may easily lead us to propose enhanced local participation and empowerment (which, by the way, is always a good thing), it is often the case that key entry points for interventions that may produce a genuine difference in the lives of local populations will be found elsewhere, be it in a capital city or even abroad.

This has several implications, including for trying to build peace (Sørbø 2015). At a time when 'localizing peace' and 'peacebuilding from below' have become fashionable as responses to the frequent failures of elite-based peace agreements, the message from anthropology is more complex. First, policymakers and peacebuilders need to pay much more attention to trying to understand developments at local levels, including what may be seen as low-intensity and localized conflicts. Such conflicts motivate violence in many countries, and peace deals made at the macro level may not trickle down to the subnational level. On the other hand, the 'local' is often fragmented and divided, and local actors are linked to external networks, including volatile client systems at different levels of scale. Local interventions may therefore be unsustainable unless linked to macro-political processes.

Second, we need to acknowledge that the situation in the Sudanese peripheries, such as in Darfur and the Nuba Mountains, has evolved over time to include both violent conflict and peaceful relations between different groups. Even during 'war', and despite the enormity of the fractures between different ethnic groups, there are mutual coping strategies by which people manage to negotiate access to natural resources, engage in trade, and sometimes even intermarry. In all of these areas, there remain local enclaves of civilian security that can be expanded to form a tangible peace in the daily lives of larger populations. For those who endure violent conflict, mitigation is, if not more valuable, at least more immediate than resolution.

The recognition of the interconnectedness of conflicts at different levels challenges the common approach to international mediation in Sudan, which has been to deal with one conflict at a time. Without understanding local and regional developments and the complex dynamics of violence, peacemakers may easily end up involuntarily fuelling existing antagonisms.

In Sudan, then, research started with a piece of applied anthropology focused on livelihoods in Darfur, the main objective being to influence decisions affecting half a million people, mostly non-Arab Fur cultivators. While this influence may have been limited, the research carried out by Barth and Haaland turned out to be both pioneering and influential in terms of advancing anthropological theory. Their insights are still relevant in terms of seeing that identities are not necessarily essential and fixed but situational, and that what counts are boundaries rather than their content.

However, as Sudan drifted towards growing violence and polarization, and as an increasingly privatized Sudanese state was used as a vehicle for special-interest groups, further stimulating divisions and processes of fragmentation, it became mandatory to analyse the larger social orders in which both ethnic identities and livelihood groups operate. While these remain important issues for basic research, investigations of this enlarged scope have also become crucial for our understanding of underlying patterns of conflict in Sudan, with important implications for all those engaged in trying to build peace in a divided and ravaged country.

A return to marginality?

While the engagement in Sudan ensured research relevance and policy orientation for those of us who were fortunate to take part in it, the international development paradigm shifted again during the mid 1980s, and the main approach shifted to focusing on creating an 'enabling environment'. At the end of the Cold War, 'getting politics right' and a concern with democracy, human rights and good governance gave political scientists a prominent role, a position that has largely been maintained as foreign and development policies increasingly merge, seen today in the preoccupation with security, fragile states and peacebuilding. In addition, small is no longer so beautiful.

These changes have also affected Norwegian aid. Thus, for example, several integrated rural development programmes in countries like Sri Lanka, Tanzania and Kenya were closed down and aid was increasingly provided in the form of sectoral programme support, particularly within health and education, often jointly with other donors. Only NGOs continued to work at local levels, but they rarely contracted anthropologists to ensure the quality of their work. If it were ever the case, the staff at Norad and the Ministry of Foreign Affairs would not secure promotion within their system by knowing something about the Nuer and Dinka in South Sudan or the Pashtuns and Tajiks in Afghanistan.

The new emphasis on macro-political developments and good governance came at a time when there were also shifts in our own discipline. A preoccupation with postmodernism made anthropology more inward looking, 'obsessed with boundary maintenance and gatekeeping' (Eriksen 2010:13). An already fragmented discipline became even more fractured, and anthropology became less visible or, as Thomas Hylland Eriksen (ibid.:23) has suggested, perhaps people out there were not terribly interested in what we were doing.

Most academic anthropologists have always had a rather detached view or, at most, only an ambiguous engagement in relation to applying anthropology to social affairs. It is no accident, I believe, that none of the metaphorically powerful ideas that earlier worked in favour of increasing the share of anthropologists in the development process (such as 'basic needs', 'adjustment with a human face' and 'farmers first') were ever coined by them. However, during the postmodernist phase, anthropologists completely failed to create even a single public agenda, at least not one that non-anthropologists found interesting.

But as the Sudan example shows, and given the state of the world and its many crises, there is a great need for ethnographically grounded research that may generate knowledge on crucial interconnections in the domains of development, democracy, rights, environment and conflict. This is not a time for complacency, and applicability does not depend on being asked or paid to write commissioned reports or working in the context of a project.

For this to happen, we should not hold a narrow view of our mission in applied or policy-oriented research, not see anthropologists as just spokespersons for the micro level, although this role is often also important. However, to move beyond the role of cultural brokers, anthropologists also have to respond to major theoretical and methodological challenges. In particular, they have to improve their ability to pursue chains of causation (or 'entanglements') that cut across the boundaries of different disciplines. In so doing, anthropologists must increase their cooperation with colleagues from other disciplines and, sometimes, become practitioners of history or political science themselves (Verdery 1994). As part of this, we must improve our ability to address issues of scale – that is, to trace trends and processes within and between regions, ecological zones and different sectors of economic and social activities.

Compared to the situation in many other countries, the relatively strong position of applied and policy-oriented research and its considerable visibility, stand out as significant features of Norwegian anthropology (Bringa and Bendixsen 2016). At the time of writing, there are several encouraging projects in which the accumulated knowledge of long-term anthropological research is being brought into direct connection and dialogue with international fields of politics and policymaking. In one case, this is being done through a broad foreign policy engagement in the Pacific, focusing on critical environmental issues regarding climate change (Hviding 2016); in another, it is being done through critical micro–macro-oriented studies related to major global crises (Eriksen 2016). Thus, although the very nature of anthropology as 'an inquisitive, challenging, uncomfortable discipline', as Raymond Firth (1981:200) put it, may pose a difficulty for its application to practical problems, there is reason to believe that large parts of the Norwegian anthropological community will avoid marginality and increasingly apply their knowledge to places where important things happen and to critical global and local interconnections.

References

Abbakar, I.A. 1985. 'Regional inequality and underdevelopment in western Sudan'. PhD thesis. Brighton: University of Sussex.

Ahmed, A.G.M. and Sørbø, G.M. 1989. 'Management of the crisis in Sudan'. Bergen: Centre for Development Studies, University of Bergen.

Barth, F. 1964. *Nomads of South Persia*. Oslo: Oslo University Press.

——— 1967a. 'Human resources: social and cultural features of the Jebel Marra Project area'. Bergen Occasional Papers in Social Anthropology No. 1. Bergen: University of Bergen.

——— 1967b. 'Economic spheres in Darfur'. In R. Firth (ed.), *Themes in Economic Anthropology*, pp. 149–74. London: Tavistock Publications.

——— 1968. 'Muligheter og begrensninger i anvendelsen av sosialantropologi på utviklingsproblemene' [Opportunities and constraints in the application of social anthropology to development problems]. *Tidsskrift for samfunnsforskning* 9(2):311–25.

——— 1970. 'Sociological aspects of integrated surveys for river basin development'. Paper presented at the Fourth International Seminar, ITC-UNESCO Centre for Integrated Surveys.

————— 1972. 'Et samfunn må forstås ut fra egne forutsetninger: U-landsforskning i sosialantropologisk perspektiv' [A society must be understood from its own circumstances: development research in anthropological perspective]. *Forskningsnytt* 17(4):7–11.

————— 1981. *Process and Form in Social Life: Selected Essays, Volume I.* London: Routledge and Kegan Paul.

————— (ed.). 1969. *Ethnic Groups and Boundaries.* Oslo: Norwegian University Press.

————— (ed.). 1978. *Scale and Social Organization.* Oslo: Norwegian University Press.

Bringa, T. and Bendixsen, S. (eds). 2016. *Engaged Anthropology: Views from Scandinavia.* New York: Palgrave.

Brox, O. 1966. *Hva skjer i Nord-Norge? En studie i norsk utkantpolitikk* [What is happening in northern Norway? A study of Norwegian policy for marginal areas]. Oslo: Pax.

————— 1971. 'Generativ planlegging' [Generative planning]. Unpublished paper, Department of Social Anthropology, University of Bergen.

————— 1991. *Praktisk samfunnsvitenskap* [Practical social science] Oslo: Universitetsforlaget.

————— 2013. 'Fra "anvendt" til anvendelig forskning?' [From 'applied' to applicable research?] *Tidsskrift for samfunnsforskning* 54(1):91–101.

de Waal, A. 2005. 'Who are the Darfurians? Arab and African identities, violence and external engagement'. *African Affairs* 104/415:181–205.

Eriksen, T.H. 2010. 'Perilous identity politics, the loss of the primitive, and an anthropology that matters: some reflections about anthropology in the new century'. In R. Costa, S. Rizvi and A. Santos (eds), *Making Sense of the Global: Anthropological Perspectives on Interconnections and Processes*, pp. 9–28. Cambridge: Cambridge Scholars Publishing.

————— 2015. *Fredrik Barth: An Intellectual Biography.* London: Pluto Press.

————— 2016. *Overheating: An Anthropology of Accelerated Change.* London: Pluto Press.

Firth, R. 1981. 'Engagement and detachment: reflections on applying social anthropology to social affairs'. *Human Organization* 40(3):193–201.

Grønhaug, R. 1978. 'Scale as a variable in analysis: fields in social organization in Herat, northwest Afghanistan'. In F. Barth (ed.), *Scale and Social Organization*, pp. 78–121. Oslo: Universitetsforlaget.

Haaland, G. 1969. 'Economic determinants in ethnic processes'. In F. Barth (ed.), *Ethnic Groups and Boundaries*, pp. 58–73. Oslo: Universitetsforlaget.

————— 1982. 'Problems of savannah development: the Sudan case'. Bergen Occasional Papers in Social Anthropology No. 19. Bergen: Department of Social Anthropology, University of Bergen.

Henriksen, G. 1974. 'Economic growth and ecological balance: problems of development in Turkana, north-western Kenya'. Bergen Occasional Papers in Social Anthropology No. 11. Bergen: Department of Social Anthropology, University of Bergen.

Howell, S. 2010. 'Norwegian academic anthropologists in public spaces'. *Current Anthropology* 51(S2):269–78.

Hviding, E. 2016. 'Europe and the Pacific: engaging anthropology in EU policy-making and development cooperation'. In T. Bringa and S. Bendixsen (eds), *Engaged Anthropology: Views from Scandinavia*, pp. 147–66. New York: Palgrave.

Kjerland, K.A. 1999. 'Kampen for å bli hørt og brukt: forholdet mellom antropologene og den norske utviklingshjelpen frem til 1987' [The fight to be heard and used: the relationship between the anthropologists and Norwegian aid until 1987]. *Historisk Tidsskrift* 3:322–46.

Klausen, A.M. 1968. *Kerala Fishermen and the Indo-Norwegian Pilot Project.* Oslo: Universitetsforlaget.

Manger, L. 2002. 'Understanding resource based conflicts and providing development in western Sudan'. Background Paper. Khartoum: United Nations Development Programme.

Popper, K. 1969. *Conjectures and Refutations.* London: Routledge.

Solheim, J. 1975. 'Er det riktig å si at moderne antropologiske forskere som Barth og Bailey "står på skuldrene til" Raymond Firth?' [Is it correct to say that modern anthropologists like Barth and Bailey are 'standing on the shoulders of' Raymond Firth?]. Unpublished paper, Department of Social Anthropology, University of Oslo.

Sørbø, G.M. 1991. 'The role of social scientists in "changing" agriculture'. In 'Natural resource use and changing society: interdisciplinary approaches to development', Proceedings of the NFU Annual Conference 1991, pp. 55–76. Aas: Agricultural University of Norway.

——— 2003. 'Pastoral ecosystems and the issue of scale'. *Ambio* 32(2):113–17.

——— 2015. 'Anthropology and peacebuilding in Sudan: some reflections'. In M.M. Assal and M.A. Abdul-Jalil (eds), *Past, Present, and Future: Fifty Years of Anthropology in Sudan*, pp. 95–110. Bergen: Chr. Michelsen Institute.

——— 2016. 'Engaging anthropology in Sudan'. In T. Bringa and S. Bendixsen (eds), *Engaged Anthropology: Views from Scandinavia*, pp. 167–82. New York: Palgrave.

Sørbø, G.M. and Ahmed, A.G.M. (eds). 2013. *Sudan Divided: Continuing Conflict in a Contested State.* New York: Palgrave MacMillan.

Takana, Y. 2016. *Darfur: Struggle of Power and Resources, 1650–2002. An Institutional Perspective.* Bergen: Chr. Michelsen Institute/Ahfad University for Women/University of Bergen.

Vayda, A. 1983. 'Progressive contextualization: methods for research in human
    ecology'. *Human Ecology* 11(3):265–81.

Verdery, K. 1994. 'Ethnicity, nationalism and state-making'. In H. Vermeulen and
    C. Govers (eds), *The Anthropology of Ethnicity: Beyond 'Ethnic Groups and
    Boundaries'*, pp. 33–58. Amsterdam: Het Spinhuis.

6

The unbearable lightness of being ... a public anthropologist in Norway

Thomas Hylland Eriksen

Milan Kundera's *The Unbearable Lightness of Being* (1984), the novel that marked the Czech author's international breakthrough and which may still win him a Nobel Prize if he lives, begins with a long rumination on Nietzsche's myth of the eternal recurrence – 'the heaviest of burdens', the absence of which renders life superficial, since everything can be forgotten and left behind with no cumulative effect if things just happen once: *Einmal ist keinmal.* The thought, which first appears in Nietzsche's *The Gay Science* (2006 [*Die fröhliche Wissenschaft*,1882]), posits that everything that happens will repeat itself again and again for eternity. As a consequence, you should invest yourself fully in everything that you do, since the event will come back, not as farce (Marx) but in its original form.

The novel juxtaposes lightness and weight: the ephemeral, fleeting and playful with that which has gravity and seriousness, imploring the reader, perhaps, to strike a balance between the two. Taking life (and yourself) too seriously is ridiculous, but not taking it seriously at all is vacuous. For Kundera (and certainly for his protagonist Tomas), love and sex stand for lightness, being fleeting and ephemeral, while weight is represented in our mortality and the irreversibility of our choices. But more fundamentally, lightness stands for the assumption that it does not matter so much what we do, since the fruit of our actions will soon be replaced and superseded by new events. The 'unbearable weight' of that 'heaviest of burdens', namely the acknowledgement of eternal recurrence, implies that all decisions and actions are profoundly significant and consequential since they will etch themselves into the memory of the world through eternal recurrence. *The Unbearable Lightness of Being* is a profound, disturbing and beautiful book that was eventually turned into an okay film (which Kundera detested).

I had just read Kundera's novel when I carried out my first ethnographic fieldwork in Mauritius in 1986, and it had no small part in my early reflections on the differences between a European sensibility and a Mauritian one, elaborated in my field notes and letters home, but never in any of my published work. Mauritians came across to me as light people with fleeting desires and a relentless optimism that contrasted with the Protestant anxiety and European ambivalence I brought with me (multicultural Mauritius has many religions, but Protestant Christianity is not one of them). The typical worries and concerns of the people I met during my first months of fieldwork seemed practical, not existential; there seemed to be anxiety without angst.

This chapter concerns the relationship between lightness and weight in Norwegian public anthropology. I have previously explored the problems of translation and relevance between anthropological analysis and the public sphere (Eriksen 2006, 2014), the problems of participation and observation when writing about minority issues in one's own country (Eriksen 2013a) and the need for anthropological knowledge in a public sphere where the demand for simple answers to complicated questions is very considerable (Eriksen 2015). What I propose to do here is compare different kinds of anthropological interventions in the Norwegian public sphere, showing that there are different ways in which we can make a difference, depending on the relationship between lightness and weight, and not least the way in which this relationship is perceived by the public.

An ambiguous social contract

> Indeed, the only truly serious questions are ones that even a child can formulate. Only the most naive of questions are truly serious. They are the questions with no answers.
>
>   —Milan Kundera, *The Unbearable Lightness of Being*

True to the prevailing instrumentalist view of knowledge, representatives of different academic disciplines sometimes speak of their 'societal assignment' (*samfunnsoppdrag*). As far as the social sciences are concerned, the economists run the country (through institutions such as the Ministry of Finance, Statistics Norway and Norway's central bank); the political scientists look after the nuts and bolts of government at all levels, from foreign policy to municipal councils; and the sociologists defend the welfare state and gender equality. What about the social anthropologists? There are many of them in Norway, which possibly has the largest proportion of anthropologists in the world. With no clearly defined professional niches, they work in many areas, from development NGOs and local government to communication agencies, libraries and the media, apart from having a wide-ranging academic presence well beyond the universities and research institutions of different kinds. A previous president of the Sámi parliament was trained as an anthropologist, as was a former minister of development.

Yet anthropology is more of a vocation than a profession. It is unclear why the country needs anthropologists, and there is an ongoing struggle to show why anthropology matters. To this end, Norwegian anthropologists have, for many years, made themselves visible in the public sphere, organizing public meetings at the popular House of Literature in Oslo, appearing on radio and TV, and writing books, essays and articles for a general readership. A subject called 'sociology and social anthropology' is the most popular optional subject in secondary school, and many Norwegians have ideas about what it is that anthropologists are and do. It is commonly assumed that anthropologists are politically radical; they are expected to defend immigrants and indigenous peoples; to criticize New Public Management and predatory capitalism; to take a distanced, sometimes ironic position on Norwegian nationalism; and to be favourable to green and leftist politics. While this is empirically simplistic – for example, the most famous Norwegian anthropologist, Fredrik Barth (1928–2016), was largely apolitical – it is not altogether wrong. Economic anthropology is very different from economic science in that it is just as preoccupied with gift exchange as with markets, just as concerned with human economy as with profitability, and when economic anthropologists study central banks or the financial crisis (Appadurai 2015; Holmes 2013), they see them as cultural systems. Political anthropology, likewise, has a long-standing interest in symbols, kinship and ritual, with power struggles often added almost as an afterthought.

In the public eye, anthropologists represent a kind of intellectual habitus that renders them susceptible to favouring small-scale egalitarian societies and cultural diversity. Yet, compared to the other social sciences, anthropologists do not have a societal assignment – *samfunnsoppdrag*. It may seem as if it were their main task to make unexpected comparisons in the public sphere, to ask unusual questions and to interrogate received wisdom. It is not our job to be worried. As a result, Norwegian anthropologists have often played the part of the trickster, like the Ash Lad (*Askeladden*) in Norwegian fairy tales (Witoszek 1998), or Anansi in West African and Caribbean lore (Eriksen 2013b).

Yet precisely because society has not provided anthropology with a set of social issues to deal with, a specified area of responsibility or a problem-solving mandate, there is a real risk of withdrawal. As elsewhere, Norwegian anthropologists are rather fond of talking amongst themselves and often forget to include the outside world in their conversations. The science fiction author Tor Åge Bringsværd once likened the relationship of society to science with the act of sending a shuttle into outer space. Society has invested money and effort into this endeavour, with the obligation on the part of the space shuttle that it should return and explain what it has seen. Too often, Bringsværd says, the space shuttle just stays out there without returning, which is a source of great disappointment for the greater public.

It is easy to sympathize with this sentiment. For what is the use of knowledge if it only circulates among the initiates? This is not to say that every anthropologist should popularize or engage in the increasingly messy meshwork that is public debate and go out and preach the gospel of anthropology to the unwashed heathens. In fact, those who do participate in these endeavours depend on those who do not; without the often arcane and difficult original research that never travels beyond seminar rooms and online university libraries, public anthropologists would have nothing to be public about. Some of the best-loved and admired Norwegian anthropologists rarely made public appearances outside the academy. One example is the late Reidar Grønhaug (1938–2005; see Vike 2010). Intellectually agile and original, generous and engaged, Grønhaug was so reticent and shy that he scarcely even published his own work, allowing unfinished research to languish in his drawer, but at least ensuring that some of his finest writings circulated among students and colleagues as mimeos. A good example is a strikingly original paper about transaction and signification (Grønhaug 1975), a spirited synthesis of Barth and Lévi-Strauss in which the centrepiece was a reanalysis of the beer-hall scene in Mitchell's famous study of the Kalela dance (1956). Many other examples could be mentioned.

The tension between the internal and the external, between openness and closure, between building knowledge and sharing it, represents a fundamental dilemma in all group dynamics. A version of the tension is wonderfully described by Sahlins in his well-known (if contested) study of political leadership in the Pacific when he outlines the structural dilemma of the Melanesian big man (Sahlins 1963).[1] In order to ensure his power base, he must spend considerable amounts of time with his relatives and supporters in the village and offer gifts to them. However, he also has to build alliances with

---

1   Incidentally, the title of Sahlins's article, 'Poor man, rich man, big man, chief', is also that of a song that has been performed at parties since the early 1990s by a group of students and junior staff from the Oslo department. The lyrics were written by Bjarne Træen, and in its most famous incarnation the band was called Pigs for the Ancestors. On a few occasions over the years, I have played a bit of sax on the song.

outsiders, mainly to prevent war and feuding, but also to extend his sphere of influence. Yet if the big man spends too much time and resources on outsiders, his kin and supporters will begin to grumble and may eventually depose him. He thus has to strike a fine balance between the internal cohesion of the group and the creation of alliances, or between consolidation and expansion.

Anthropologists who have gone out of their way to communicate with a non-anthropological audience have often been reminded of the truth of Sahlins's simple analysis. If you go out, you may flourish and it may enrich your own people by making them more famous and attractive to others; but, if you start doing business with outsiders before paying your debts at home, it may also be your own undoing.

For a long time, Norwegian anthropologists have taken their chances with this balance. What sets Norwegian anthropology apart is not only that anthropologists are pretty thick on the ground (see Bendixsen, this volume), but also that they are a familiar sight, individually and collectively, in the public sphere. Only in the week before this chapter was initially presented at the RAI's Norwegian Anthropology Day, we were reminded of the Norwegian readership's familiarity with anthropology by the financial daily *Dagens Næringsliv*. Their Saturday supplement featured a six-page long interview with the anthropologist Tone Danielsen, who had recently defended her doctoral thesis (Danielsen 2015). Her research, based on long-term fieldwork among soldiers, concerned the socialization, rituals and group identity emerging from the Norwegian Naval Special Operation Commandos during their long and strenuous training programme.

In writing a portrait of Danielsen and discussing her work with her, the journalist did not at any point need to explain what social anthropology is to his intended readership. He could safely assume that they had some general ideas that the discipline involves the study of small groups through participant observation, that anthropologists have a weakness for culture and rituals, and that they nowadays study any kind of small group – vegans, stockbrokers, religious sects – as though they were a primitive tribe. This all went without saying. After all, Norwegian anthropologists go on the radio and show up in the newspapers every year before Christmas explaining the logic of gift exchange, often with a sideways glance to the potlatch and Melanesia; when spring comes, they comment on the rituals and symbols of football supporters; around Easter, they may write or talk about the peculiar Norwegian habit of spending Easter skiing in the mountains; and in autumn, they may take part in more serious discussions about the significance of the Muslim headscarf in Norway's growing Muslim minority. They risk becoming academic court jesters, but they may equally well be those who can speak truth to power because they have no vested interests. There is both lightness and gravity in the work of the public anthropologist. Let me now turn to a few brief examples.

The light and the heavy

> Tomas did not realize at the time that metaphors are dangerous. Metaphors are not to be trifled with. A single metaphor can give birth to love.
> —Milan Kundera, *The Unbearable Lightness of Being*

Many public interventions by anthropologists are decidedly on the heavy side. They deal with matters of existential gravity in an unequivocally serious way. For example, there is no lightness in Aud Talle's short book about female circumcision (Talle 2003), which explains the social and cultural logic behind the custom, its variations and the ways in which one might combat it. Nor is there much jocularity in Unni Wikan's critique of patriarchy and religious conservatism among Muslim immigrants (Wikan 1995) – a critique which, unsurprisingly, led to prolonged debate among Norwegian anthropologists, several of whom disagreed publicly with Wikan. Nor, for that matter, is their much levity in Marianne Gullestad's research on Norwegian racism (Gullestad 2002, 2006), which alleges that racist exclusion is far more widespread than often assumed, but is usually invisible because it is implicit and embodied rather than articulated and verbalized. These interventions, all of which were widely disseminated and discussed in the media and among elites, have little of the lightness described by Kundera – as those fleeting, superficial, passing events and emotions that leave little trace but make up much of our lives.

For the present purpose, a different kind of intervention is more interesting – namely those that can perhaps easily be perceived as light, but which juxtapose lightness with weight, and shift between hyperbole, naturalism and surrealism. An anthropologist specializing in food and consumption, Runar Døving, wrote his doctoral dissertation about change and continuity in the food habits of a small hamlet in south-eastern Norway. Active in the public sphere at the time of his research, he wrote an op-ed in the Oslo newspaper *Dagbladet*, in which he strongly defended the hot dog against its detractors. Without mentioning Bourdieu once, Døving (2002) persuasively and convincingly attacked food snobbery and the new culinary distinctions resulting from the individualization and differentiation usually associated with neoliberal deregulation. The piece was written with verve and passion, it was light-hearted and fun to read, yet at the same time it was serious and heavy. Tracing the development of food processing from pre-modern to industrial times, Døving points out that the mass-produced food of today, jeered at by culinary elites, is tastier and more wholesome than the unique and painstakingly hand-made food romanticized by food snobs. In fact, he says, the contemporary abundance of industrially produced food ought to be celebrated, considering the food scarcities and hard work entailed by food production just a couple of generations ago. He then goes on to describe how children then had to contribute to food production, how that expensive luxury called butter was distributed in open, unhygienic containers (and went stale quickly) and how fathers had to work fifty hours a week while mothers and the oldest children spent the afternoons salting herring. In a word, Døving's seemingly light-hearted defence of the hot dog 'with that exciting tomato sauce, the ketchup' was a bitter critique of new class distinctions and a defence of the achievements of modern food production. One of his best op-eds to date, the article summarized a small library of recent debates in the anthropology of food parading as a defence of hot dogs, fish pudding and tinned mackerel.

Some years earlier, the anthropologist Hans Christian Sørhaug carried out an applied research project on drug addicts in Oslo (Sørhaug 1988). One of his findings was that they could be compared to hunters and gatherers: Their storage capacity was low, they relied on immediate returns from investment, they were itinerant, group size was flexible but small, and there was a continuous, accepted tension between egotism and solidarity. Theirs was a 'harvesting economy'. This discovery was genuine and original, and contributed to a deepened understanding of the plight of the heroin addicts of the city. Yet the comparison might be perceived as light-hearted, almost facetious. After all, the society in which drug addicts live, and the forces that have created their situation, are very different from the world of hunters and gatherers, and in order to appreciate the comparison, one has to bracket prior assumptions about cultural differences. You have to be able to switch between a playful mode exploring options and lifeworlds, and a serious concern with the plight of homeless heroin addicts.

Similarly, Eduardo Archetti was interviewed by the Oslo newspaper *Aftenposten* some time in the 1990s about the prolonged graduation partying that takes place among Norwegian teenagers after leaving school. A unique tradition, these celebrations, which are known locally as *russefeiring* (see Eriksen 2013b for details), are characterized by alcohol and frivolous partying in parks and other public spaces and last for more than two weeks, from May Day to Constitution Day, 17 May, when the celebrations reach a climax of sorts. Asked about this ritual, Archetti, himself the father of two teenage children at the time, responded that this was a powerful and meaningful experience for young people, not least since it was the first time that many of them participated in rituals that involved sex and intoxicating substances. It may safely be assumed that more than a few anxious parents did not find his comments reassuring. The point is nevertheless that Archetti did not see it as his assigned task to act the part of the worried social scientist, to tell the parents, say, that it was important that they stay awake and have a good chat with their children when they returned home from the day's partying, or that girls should never walk home alone in a drunken state. His job was to view the graduation celebrations as a ritual, not as a social problem.

I have briefly spoken of six anthropological interventions in the public sphere. The first three are easy to see as attempts to act as critical intellectuals drawing on empirical knowledge to explain features of the world and as contributions to a larger conversation about the state of society and what should be done about it. The last three – Døving, Sørhaug, and Archetti – have not conducted long-term research on the issues at hand (on the contrary, two of the examples are brief newspaper items), but represent a more complex rhetorical position in which the intended *logos* risks being drowned out by the perceived *pathos*. Although serious in intent, the latter three all reveal a light, playful dimension as well, even involving a perceptible jocularity. They have embarked on a risky journey, but one that is arguably more common among social anthropologists than in any other academic profession in the country. The risk consists in not being taken seriously because people only remember the jokes and not their context. This is a familiar problem for political satire (if it is too funny, people forget that it is serious) and for science fiction (superficial readers remember the technology but not the philosophical insights), and similarly, anthropologists who expose their comparative imagination in public risk being written off as irresponsible dilettantes. Yet it is an open question whether this somewhat indeterminate aspect of public anthropology is ultimately a problem or an advantage.

Anarchists of Western academia

> On the surface, an intelligible lie; underneath, the unintelligible truth.
> —Milan Kundera, *The Unbearable Lightness of Being*

The times have changed since the turn of the millennium. Norwegian anthropologists, the anarchists of academia, have occasionally found themselves being co-opted by the entertainment industry in the recent past. More than once, some of us have been accused of having become 'a song and dance man'. Although the spirit of the times has changed in this century, and there is less room for irresponsible play with ideas than at the height of postmodernist optimism in the 1990s, anthropologists can still, on a good day, be counted on to say weird or unexpected things. Yet today, at a time of rising Islamophobia (currently represented in Norway by the government), difficult refugee issues, rampant marketization and an instrumentalist view of knowledge that works in tandem with New Public Management to threaten the freedom of universities, the lightness of the recent past, of which I have given a few examples, has almost faded from sight. Although there is a serious underlying concern below the lightness I have depicted – Døving was concerned with class, Archetti with the pains and excitement of becoming an adult, Sørhaug with the double-binds and illusions of absolute freedom among drug addicts – it seemed harmless and indeed legitimate to play the part of Anansi the spider.

A dreadful reminder of the fact that lightness can become unbearable came to me in a rather personal way a few years ago. Ideological polarization had already developed for some time, fanned by the Islamic terrorist attacks in New York, London and Madrid, and social anthropologists were increasingly being associated with a naive multiculturalism gone awry. For many years, some of us had questioned social boundaries, asking critical questions with a bearing on the ethnic dimension of Norwegian nationalism. Then, at the height of summer in 2011, a bomb exploded. The majority that anthropologists had been busy deconstructing should now be reconstructed, and violent means were deemed necessary to this end.

As a matter of fact, 'deconstructing the majority' has become something of a catchword in Norway after the terrorist attack in 2011, when an unemployed right-wing extremist killed seventy-seven people. In his manifesto and YouTube video – posted online immediately before the attack – he quoted me in several places, the most notorious quotation (which has subsequently appeared on right-wing websites worldwide) being my view, taken from an interview on an obscure University of Oslo website, that it was about time that we deconstructed the majority, since we had devoted so much attention to minorities.[2] Before and after the terrorist attack, this statement (from 2009) has often been denounced as hate speech against the Norwegian people, its originator labelled a traitor. In a word, when I spoke about deconstructing the majority, I misjudged the readership. In the interview I questioned the self–other boundary and pointed to internal diversity among ethnic Norwegians as a possible means to build an abstract or imagined community not based on race and kinship. Since deconstruction refers to taking something apart, ethnic nationalists, worried about their boundaries, felt threatened. However, even in the cheerful 1990s, when Norwegian anthropologists like myself made fun of earnest, flag-waving nationalism, the topic was deadly serious. Behind

---

2   The interview in question was for years available at www.uio.no/culcom, but this increasingly obsolete website has been renovated and reduced, and the interview is now gone.

the jokes, we intended to raise questions about inclusion and exclusion in ethnically complex societies, asking whether ethnic nationalism was a helpful vehicle of identity in a world where 'most of us are on the move even if physically, bodily, we stay put' (Bauman 1998:77), and, ultimately, asking what a meaningful delineation of the word 'we' might be. The message, normative but founded on anthropological knowledge about cultural diversity, was that all human lives have value, that solidarity with others does not necessarily follow ethnic lines, that imagined communities are less homogeneous than often assumed and that a collective identity not based on cultural similarity was perfectly imaginable and could be feasible. Following the terrorist attack and an increasing ideological polarization around questions of identity and inclusion in Norwegian society, the lightness typical of an anthropology of the recent past may have been one of the first casualties.

This is a shame because, as I hope I have indicated, anthropology can be at its heaviest when it is at its lightest. Kundera, not a writer to eschew paradoxes, might nod in agreement. Solving problems for the government has never been our strongest contribution, nor can anthropologists ever dream of competing with other academic disciplines when it comes to worrying about the future of society.

Finding a space between Scylla and Charybdis

> A person who longs to leave the place where he lives is an unhappy person.
> —Milan Kundera, *The Unbearable Lightness of Being*

(Or perhaps he or she is just a social anthropologist.)

Since problem-solving for the government and corporations are not options, anthropologists have to find other ways of being relevant – or, as Tian Sørhaug once said, true to the light/heavy duality of the public anthropologist's trade, 'we've always been irrelevant, but it seems that we have to find new ways of being irrelevant these days'. There has been a shift towards a more aggressive, uncharitable and hostile view of cultural diversity in dominant parts of society, and this shift requires that public anthropologists change their tactics. Since some version of social anthropology is already known in the Norwegian public sphere, the problem is not so much – as it might have been in the 1960s and 1970s – that people out there do not understand what anthropologists are saying; they understand it perfectly well and dismiss it as irrelevant (in the wrong way) and as potentially subversive. Accordingly, it is more difficult to produce the kinds of discussion that might have been productive before the recent shift towards a stronger assertion of boundaries and a more conservative view of identity.

It is beyond the scope of this short chapter to solve these issues. I would instead like to conclude by reminding the reader that there are two trenches to be avoided, namely oversimplification and obscurantism. This should be the overarching aim of public anthropology – making it as simple as possible, but not simpler (as Einstein reputedly said); encourage imagination, but not confusion. The currently dominant knowledge regime prioritizes not only instrumentally useful knowledge (useful, that is, for the powers that be, mainly in politics and the economy) but also anything that can be measured (Eriksen 2015). Since our strength lies in producing knowledge about phenomena that cannot easily be counted or measured, anthropologists have to make an effort to show the relevance of our irrelevant knowledge. Equally, if nobody understands what we are saying, that is not an indication of profundity, but of poor language skills and muddled thought. As Marshall McLuhan once put it, 'even mud can give the illusion of depth'.

We can be sand in the machinery, but we can also open up new vistas. And we have to take the problem of translation seriously. It is never easy, but anthropologists are supposed to have an advantage in this area. When you say 'deconstruction', your students and colleagues hear one thing, while an uneducated and spiteful man hears something else. This needs to be kept in mind. In today's world, alas, we have to consider the range of possible misunderstandings before going on air. *Traduttore e traditore* – the translator is a traitor – and for a long time, I was convinced that being misunderstood was better than not being understood at all. Now, I am not so sure. Some time ago, I came across a photo of a label on a garment that read, in Norwegian, *Laget i Kalkun*. Trying, perhaps, to save money, the manufacturers must have used Google Translate to render 'Made in Turkey' into Norwegian. The only problem is that *kalkun* does not designate a country, but an oversized, flightless bird that is known in Spanish as *pavo*, in French as *dinde* and in German as *Truthahn* or *Truthuhn*, depending on the bird's gender. When the simplest of translations can lead to such catastrophic consequences, it almost stands to reason that anthropologists are loath to render their own insights and those of their colleagues in ordinary language. But only almost. We must keep trying.

References

Appadurai, A. 2015. *Banking on Words: The Failure of Language in the Age of Derivative Finance*. Chicago: University of Chicago Press.

Bauman, Z. 1998. *Globalization: The Human Consequences*. Cambridge: Polity Press.

Danielsen, T. 2015. 'Making warriors in the global era – an anthropological study of institutional apprenticeship: selection, training, education and everyday life in the Norwegian Naval Special Operations Commando'. PhD thesis. Oslo: University of Oslo.

Døving, R. 2002. 'Kjendiskokker og ketchuphat' [Celebrity chefs and ketchup hatred]. *Dagbladet*, 9 February. Available at: www.dagbladet.no/kultur/ kjendiskokker-og-ketchup-hat/65785363 (accessed 30 October 2017).

Eriksen, T.H. 2006. *Engaging Anthropology: The Case for a Public Presence*. Oxford: Berg.

——— 2013a. 'Norwegian anthropologists study minorities at home: political and academic agendas'. In S. Beck and C. Maida (eds), *Toward Engaged Anthropology*, pp. 36–54. Oxford: Berghahn Books.

——— 2013b. 'The Anansi position'. *Anthropology Today* 29(6):14–17 .

——— 2014. 'Public anthropology'. In H.R. Bernard and C.C. Gravlee (eds), *Handbook of Methods in Cultural Anthropology*, pp. 719–34. Lanham, MD: Rowman and Littlefield.

——— 2015. 'What everybody should know about nature-culture: anthropology in the public sphere and "the two cultures"'. In S. Beck and C. Maida (eds), *Public Anthropology in a Borderless World*, pp. 264–85. Oxford: Berghahn Books.

Grønhaug, R. 1975. 'Transaction and signification'. Unpublished paper. University of Bergen.

Gullestad, M. 2002. *Det Norske Sett med Nye Øyne: Kritisk Analyse av Norsk Innvandringsdebatt* [Norwegianness from a new perspective: critical analysis of the Norwegian immigration debate]. Oslo: Universitetsforlaget.

——— 2006. *Plausible Prejudice: Everyday Experiences and Social Images of Nation, Culture and Race*. Oslo: Scandinavian University Press.

Holmes, D. 2013. *Economy of Words: Communicative Imperatives in Central Banks*. Chicago: University of Chicago Press.

Kundera, M. 1984. *The Unbearable Lightness of Being*. New York: Harper and Row.

Mitchell, J.C. 1956. 'The Kalela dance: aspects of social relationships among urban Africans in Northern Rhodesia'. Rhodes-Livingstone Paper No. 27. Manchester: Manchester University Press.

Nietzsche, F. 2006 [1882]. *The Gay Science*. Dover Publications.

Sahlins, M. 1963. 'Poor man, rich man, big man, chief: political types in Melanesia and Polynesia'. *Comparative Studies in Society and History* 5:285–303.

Sørhaug, H. C. 1988. Identitet. Grenser, autonomi og avhengighet – stoffmisbruk som eksempel [Identity: Boundaries, autonomy and addiction – substance abuse as a case]. *Alkoholpolitikk - Tidsskrift for nordisk alkoholforskning*, **5**: 31-39.

Talle, A. 2003. *Om Kvinneleg Omskjering: Debatt og Erfaring* [On female circumcision: debate and experience]. Oslo: Det Norske Samlaget.

Vike, H. 2010. 'Reidar Grønhaugs metode: en kraftlinje i norsk sosialantropologi'
[Reidar Grønhaug's method: a line of power in Norwegian social
anthropology]. *Norsk Antropologisk Tidsskrift* 21:211–22.

Wikan, U. 1995. *Mot en Ny Norsk Underklasse: Innvandrere, Kultur og Integrasjon*
[Towards a new Norwegian underclass: immigrants, culture and
integration]. Oslo: Gyldendal.

Witoszek, N. 1998. *Norske Naturmytologier: Fra Edda til Økofilosofi* [Norwegian
nature mythologies: from the Eddas to ecophilosophy]. Oslo: Pax.

7

Disagreement, illumination and mystery

Towards an ethnography of anthropology in Norway

Synnøve Bendixsen

Introduction

This chapter invites the readers to learn about the life of a particular group
of people, namely anthropologists in Norway. In this brief ethnographic
description of the people, I provide insight into their behaviour as scientists,
their forms of engagement in a political and economic environment
characterized by neoliberalism, and their recent paths taken to ensure the
survival and flourishing of their ideas and practices, as a discipline. The
exceptionality of Norwegian anthropology can be illustrated not merely by
the number of qualified practitioners and calls for interviews from journalists
and radio hosts, but also by their visible public presence and their resilience
in terms of continuing to conduct long-term fieldwork – a practice which is
today considered unreasonably time-consuming in the high-pressure, New
Public Management context of university life and knowledge production.
What is current anthropology in Norway? Who are its people? How are they
surviving in an increasingly harsh neoliberal environment?

I will discuss this particular group of people and their relations of
production through an account of disagreement, illumination and local
knowledge production at the margin. By examining this people's considerable
(and growing) diversity over the past fifteen years, I seek to cast light on what
may seem enigmatic to outsiders: the mystery of how this group of people
that we call 'anthropologists in Norway' has managed to survive and flourish
through global economic crises, university reorganization, changes of funding
criteria and the like.

Having pursued most of my anthropological graduate studies abroad, my perspective is that of an insider-outsider, although I am increasingly becoming native through institutional employment in Norway. The data on which I base this brief ethnographic account is from my experiences as an undergraduate student in 1997, as a post-doctoral fellow at the University of Bergen from 2014 to 2018, and from internet sources, conversations in the Bergen department's hallways and elsewhere, and the many publications by group members. After a short introduction to the group, anthropologists in Norway, I turn to a discussion of their relations of production and their rituals of verification. I subsequently discuss how an external evaluation of anthropologists in Norway showed the way to a gift from the Research Council of Norway (RCN), which has subsequently contributed to important – and fortunately long-lasting – debates over what kinds of anthropology should best be pursued. Finally, I present an informal and incomplete overview of this group's local knowledge production over the last fifteen years.

Introducing the people

According to a national newspaper, Norway is the country in the world with the most social anthropologists per capita – in fact around one anthropologist per two thousand inhabitants. You might meet someone with a background in anthropology in the most surprising of places – not only in directly relevant areas of work but in such professions as journalism, the civil service, politics and the police. Even Norway's current crown princess, Mette-Marit, studied social anthropology for a while at the University of Oslo, prior to her marriage to the prince. Anthropology is taught as a discipline at all levels at four of Norway's universities – in Oslo, Bergen, Trondheim and Tromsø – with the Oslo and Bergen departments being the largest with about fifteen permanent faculty each. Considering combined numbers from all four departments at the time of the RAI's Norwegian Anthropology Day, there were approximately eighty-two anthropologists studying for a doctorate and 180 master's students. This pattern persists. A considerable number of anthropologists, moreover, work not in university departments but at various research institutes and regional colleges, and in a great diversity of non-academic professions around the country. Taken together, Norwegian anthropologists live and work in particular configurations of relations of production, involving dimensions of scale, university structure and funding opportunities, all of which shape social relations and knowledge formation.

Relations of production

The sheer number, size, geographical dispersity of anthropological departments in this country, together with an historical tradition of different categories of charismatic authorities working from the local territories, have perhaps contributed to the growth and flourishing of subsystems, prevented hegemonic theoretical routes and facilitated the growth of multiple themes and analytical approaches. Research groups are often constituted through externally-funded projects – such as Pacific studies, egalitarianism and Eurasian borderlands in Bergen, and 'overheating' and cultures of biodiversity in Oslo – have brought together master's and doctoral students, post-doctoral fellows and permanent faculty in thematically and/or geographically focused structures of vertical integration. At the same time, academic reproduction is generated through the departments' regular teaching of mainstream anthropological topics. Goffman's distinction between backstage and frontstage in the presentation of self (Goffman 1959) provides a constructive framework for thinking about these relations: students are introduced to established canons of anthropology by lecturers and professors who, after giving these lectures, withdraw to pursue their peculiar, or perhaps also classic, research interests, be they headhunters or the becoming of salmon. Thus the frontstage of anthropology in Norway remains rather homogeneous and ensures the continuity of the discipline, whereas the backstage remains diversified.

This dual process has intensified since 2003, when the neoliberal state's sledgehammer instructed Norwegian universities to produce and teach modules of formalized subjects with associated credit points, thereby securing income to departments based on the 'production' of credit points through students' successful exams. Department faculty collectively composed anthropological canons that they found acceptable or at least could live with. A comparison of the undergraduate reading lists of the Bergen and Oslo departments indicate general agreement on the most important content. Meanwhile, the very stability of this canon-based teaching requirement enabled researchers to pursue their individual, disciplinary passions backstage.

Social anthropology in Norway has grown steadily since the 1960s (see Smedal, this volume), with a rapidly accelerated growth rate in the 1990s, boosted by the state's channelling of unemployed youth through the university system. From oral traditions of that time I have learned that bachelor courses in Oslo were taught in the huge, venerable Colosseum Cinema, since the largest university auditoriums – with room for 400 people – were simply too small. In today's departments, every permanent faculty member is expected to teach all subjects offered, and as a rule advertised permanent positions require a strong background in mainstream social anthropology. New lecturers or professors are recruited as potential generalists, yet evaluated as specialists – although situated within a broader holistically oriented anthropology. Thus, while reproducing the discipline frontstage through teaching, anthropologists in Norway are further cultivating and diversifying the discipline in their research backstage, whilst at the same time being notably defiant at the margins of frontstage through the intensive teaching of so-called *con amore* courses that offer glimpses of ongoing specialist research.

Subversiveness through research is achieved by means of various external sources of funding, including the Research Council of Norway (RCN) and the European Commission. While funding calls from the RCN and the EU have moved in the direction of advocating more 'applied research' with 'societal impact', the proposals submitted by Norwegian anthropologists tend to have quite a high rate of success, despite being frequently thematically (and geographically) exotic. This brings to mind to Fredrik Barth's well-known attitude introduced long ago: 'There is no such thing as basic and applied research – what we are talking about is solid basic research that will sooner or later be applied, and poor research that should never be applied any way'.[1] My own current fieldwork base, the Department of Social Anthropology in Bergen, actually has long maintained the largest portfolio of externally funded research projects in the university's entire Faculty of Social Sciences. For example, the Bergen Pacific studies group was awarded 10 million kroner (approximately 1 million GBP) in 2008 for no-strings-attached comparative field research in Melanesia, Polynesia and Micronesia.

In 2015, two European Research Council (ERC) Advanced Grant projects (each worth about 25 million kroner) were operative: 'Overheating' led by Thomas Hylland Eriksen in the Oslo department, and in the Bergen Department, 'Egalitarianism' led by Bruce Kapferer. Both projects were designed to take the pulse of the contemporary world through globally wide-ranging fieldwork and comparative analysis. In 2018 the Bergen department received a grant of 25 million kroner from the RCN's Toppforsk programme to undertake comparative and interdisciplinary research led by Edvard Hviding on sea-level rise and maritime sovereignty in the Pacific. In 2019 the Oslo department received an ERC Starting Grant for a comparative study of connections between the global ocean and four major ports, led by Elisabeth Schober. These are just glimpses of what by any standard is a successful, ongoing record of securing major grants for Norwegian anthropology.

Social relations across the four Norwegian anthropology departments are kept alive through the regular use of external examiners for master's theses,

---

1   The remarks are from a speech given in Norwegian by Barth at the opening ceremony for the University of Bergen's Centre for Development Studies in 1986. The Norwegian original: *Det er ikke noe som heter grunnforskning og anvendt forskning – hva det er snakk om er solid forskning som før eller senere blir anvendt, og dårlig forskning som aldri bør anvendes.* Thanks to Gunnar M. Sørbø (personal communication) for sharing them with me.

and by the annual conferences of the Norwegian Anthropological Association that alternate between the cities of the four departments. These regularized events spark off dialogues and consolidate webs of connection among anthropologists inside and outside academia.

Rituals of verification

The 'new managerialism' of accountability seen as a pervasive aspect of neoliberal governmentality has also become a taken-for-granted practice of the Norwegian government, which is the owner of the universities at which anthropology is taught. Neoliberal audit culture – which has the character of a disciplining exercise, 'helping (monitoring) people help (monitor) themselves' (Strathern 2000:4) – has been transferred from the private corporate to the public sector, including the domain of higher education. With the explosion of audit systems, all university disciplines have been drawn deeply into new agendas of managerial practice. In 2010, the time came for Norwegian social anthropology to experience the system's specific ritual of verification: the machinery of evaluation.

After a prolonged process of investigation, the external audit conducted by an international panel of anthropologists reported that anthropology should certainly be considered a vibrant and high-profile discipline in Norway today. The complexity of empirical ethnographic material that Barth (1989) once argued was a principal characteristic of anthropology in Norway was duly recognized by the panel's evaluation report, which stated that: 'The most profound legacy [of anthropology in Norway] is a strong emphasis on original ethnographic research, which is still remarkable' (Hastrup *et al.* 2011:7). However, the report also noted that 'the founding fathers also still stand as figures that are hard to circumvent entirely' (ibid.:21).

Not surprisingly, this 'independent expert report' also emphasized a need for self-improvement to realize the potential of the field. Its authors argued that there was 'a certain lack of ambition with respect to the international development of anthropological theory and method' (ibid.:7). Thus anthropologists in Norway should aim to become more visible internationally, particularly in terms of developing theory. Despite this assessment, however, in my own, albeit limited, ethnographic research on anthropologists in Norway, I have noted high numbers of international publications among the population in question, and also observed that it is increasingly common for younger scholars to publish revisions of their doctoral theses as monographs with international presses of high repute.

Perhaps only in Norway – a place where the state is still wealthy – can a disciplining exercise of deep governmentality create a pool of more research money dedicated to facilitate further improvements in the performance indicators of evaluated departments, centres and research groups. Five prominent representatives of Norwegian institutional anthropology were recruited by the RCN to form a committee for 'evaluation follow-up', and this committee duly submitted a report on proposed national priorities; this in turn resulted in the allocation of a gift consisting of 12 million kroner by the RCN in 2012 as a commitment to the post-evaluation development of the discipline. Following a call and a number of submitted applications, the funds were distributed to four so-called 'institution-based strategic projects' (ISP), a fifth being one of national collaboration in PhD training. Three of these four-year ISP projects were based in anthropology departments (the universities of Bergen, Oslo and Trondheim), and their titles are instructive for discerning some patterns. The Bergen ISP was 'Denaturalizing difference: challenging the production of global social inequality'; in Oslo, the ISP was 'Anthropos and the material: challenges to anthropology'; and the Trondheim ISP was 'Global social inequality and the anthropology of uncertainty, contingency and future orientation'. It is worth noting both contrasts and overlaps in these titles. All three projects had stated ambitions concerning the development of anthropological theory; they were linked to processes of inequality and difference at various scales; and they proposed exploring these issues comparatively by assessing and elaborating on ethnographic materials that had already been collected worldwide by the faculty of each department. There was also considerable cross-departmental participation in each ISP, particularly between Oslo and Bergen.

This generous gift from the RCN was far from unwelcome, as it facilitated a very wide range of diverse opportunities for publication, seminars and conferences. The approximately 3 million kroner allocated by the RCN to each departmental ISP in fact did not include research salaries; rather, the money was destined for national and international conferences and other forms of collaboration both near and far, research assistance, visiting fellowships for international colleagues, editorial work, publishing and similar 'infrastructural' dimensions. The inception and realization of the Norwegian Anthropology Day (and ultimately the present volume) were in fact built into the application for the Bergen ISP from the beginning, and as such the entire event was funded by the gift from the RCN to the Bergen department. The ISP funding also enabled a dedicated drive towards ensuring international publications, including a recent edited volume from the Oslo ISP (Harvey *et al.* 2019) and the Palgrave MacMillan series 'Approaches to social inequality and difference' (established and managed by the editors of this volume), dedicated to comparative anthropological studies of various forms of social inequality produced in global social and political formations, and which by 2019 had seen the publication of nine volumes.[2]

As anthropologists surely know very well, a gift always comes with the expectations of a subsequent return. And so, in return for their gift, the RCN asked for greater engagement by Norway's institutional anthropological community in the development of anthropological theory, the strengthening of collaboration across Norwegian institutions and overall a more internationally visible Norwegian anthropology. Notably, however, the RCN called for no further ethnographic fieldwork, although this was viewed by the evaluation as the discipline's most enduring strength. The foundational nature of this gift – or, alternatively, the RCN's investment – did create some ambivalence among Norway's anthropologists and fuelled both existing and new critical debates.

Disagreements and illuminations

As part of the post-evaluation investment in anthropology, resources were channelled to the organization of high-profile national debates at the annual Norwegian Anthropological Association conference, inspired by the Group for Debates in Anthropological Theory at the University of Manchester, albeit with distinctive local characteristics. With two speakers arguing for and two against a specific motion, the Norwegian debates illustrated how anthropologists related in diverse and often conflicting ways to contemporary issues involving the nature and scope of foundational principles. At the 2013 conference (in Oslo) the motion was: 'There is no doubt that ANT [actor–network theory] and material semiotics are a field of knowledge one must relate to as an anthropologist'. The motion for the 2014 debate (held in Bergen) was: 'Today's theory development is a threat to the distinctiveness of Norwegian anthropology'; and in 2015 (in Trondheim) the title was: 'Without "the Other", no anthropology'. These three debates were published in their entirety (in Norwegian) in the peer-reviewed national anthropological journal, *Norsk Antropologisk Tidsskrift*.

The three motions chosen reflect discussions spurred by the audit process and subsequent ISP funding. Some anthropologists worried that an increased internationalization of theoretical engagement would throw the baby out with the bathwater: being, and becoming, too bent on closely following theoretical developments in the centre (for which read: the United States and the United Kingdom) could undermine Norway's strength of working at the margins, and thus contribute to peripheralizing anthropology in Norway. In that regard, naturalized Norwegian anthropologist Bruce Kapferer argued in an interview published in 2012:

---

2   For Palgrave Macmillan series, see www.palgrave.com/gp/series/14775.

[a]nthropology was a discipline of the periphery that gained its energy in the periphery. It's *in* the periphery that you actually are able to place the centre in some sort of critical relation. So Norway is important to anthropology, a great place from which to critically reflect on the metropolis.

(quoted in Bertelsen 2012:195)

For example, while several prominent Norwegian anthropologists speaking in the debates perceived ANT and the ontological turn as old wine in new bottles, most agreed that dismissing theoretical developments altogether would create a myth that anthropologists in Norway have solved the riddle of how to conduct 'real anthropology'. Such a myth about a consummated anthropology would amount to a conservative mind-set and disregard the widely shared perception that how to pursue theory, and what kind of theory, in anthropology remains ever open for debate.

Another enduring source of disagreement and illumination, as intellectual enlightenment, concerns the characteristics and future of fieldwork as the particular strength of anthropology in Norway. Some fear that in a time of result-oriented and fast-track education, fewer students will pursue long-term fieldwork outside Western countries, or indeed outside urbanized neighbourhoods. The existence of this fear brings to mind the idea that fieldwork in Norway is second-rate, based on the assumption that 'home blindness' (see Vike 2018 for a critique) eliminates the analytical distance needed for good research – an argument to which I return when discussing local knowledge. What numbers in fact show is that in Oslo and Bergen, 70 to 80 per cent of master's students still conduct their fieldwork outside Norway and the rest of Europe. Among doctoral candidates in Bergen, a recent quick survey I did indicated that a mere 15 per cent conduct fieldwork in Norway. Thus, relatively speaking, an overwhelmingly high percentage of students still conduct their fieldwork abroad. Granted, master's students are today expected to spend six months in the field and no more – nonetheless, Malinowski's archetype is still the idealized model before, during and after fieldwork.

As we see, the external observations of the evaluation and audit process initiated an internal process of self-scrutiny and self-observation – bringing the discipline to task – a causative pattern that seems to lie at the heart of audit culture. Clearly, this also represents a continuation of the anthropological ethos – internal criticism and self-accountability have always been part and parcel of social anthropology (Argyrou 2000). I will finally discuss what can be considered to be this group's local knowledge, or what is their knowledge production at the margins.

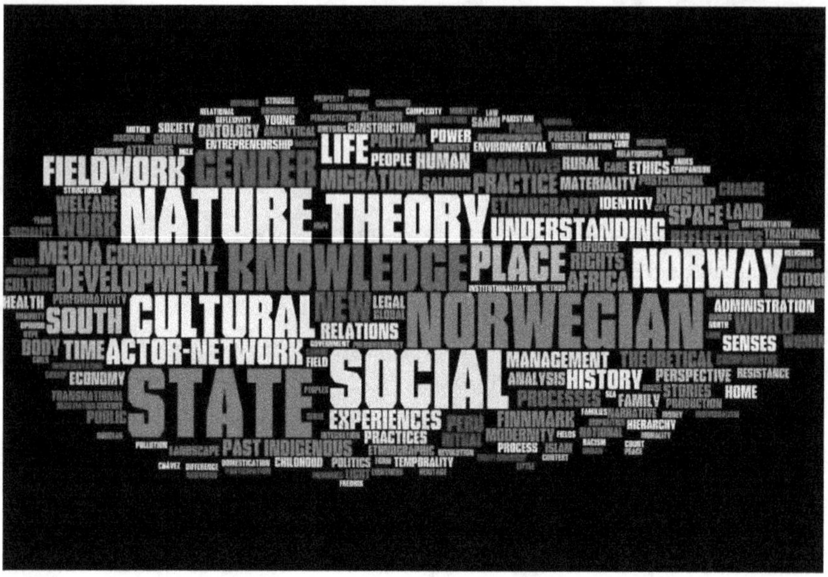

Figure 7.1 Word cloud.

Local knowledge

Most anthropologists in Norway are members of the Norwegian Anthropological Association and thus subscribe to a peer-reviewed vernacular journal by the name of *Norsk Antropologisk Tidsskrift* (*NAT*). It was founded in 1990, has continued to publish four volumes a year, and in 2017 went open-access and fully online. The journal functions as an *agora*, and in addition to peer-reviewed articles it publishes a variety of discussion pieces across genres. At home in Norway, it has remained the discipline's only shared written academic forum, also constituting an arena for novices to publish their first article – and it has been crucial in maintaining and developing a Norwegian anthropological jargon.

Collecting article headlines from *NAT* from 2002 to 2015 and each article's stated keywords from 2007 to 2015, I have made use of the methodologically dubious tool – or rather toy – of 'word clouds', which gives greater visual prominence to words that appear more frequently in the source corpus. Obviously, no single journal reflects or intends to reflect an entire discipline. Yet headlines and keywords point to cryptic, condensed metanarratives offering an opportunity to reflect on directions in anthropological research over the past decade. This, then, is the image of anthropology in Norway provided by my gathering.

For a journal publishing exclusively in the Norwegian language (very rare exceptions being pieces in Danish, Swedish or English), it should come as no surprise that 'Norway' and 'Norwegian' emerge substantially in the word cloud.

Keywords such as 'state', 'nature', 'cultural', 'social', 'knowledge', 'fieldwork' and 'development' also stand out. In addition, there is also a small 'Fredrik' (could it be Fredrik Barth?) in the left-hand corner, as well as 'Finnmark', 'salmon' and 'migration'. Behind the multiplicity of these keywords is the specificity of scholarship conducted in Norway, which is what I want to reflect upon finally.

Until the early twenty-first century, anthropological studies in Norway rarely focused on mainstream Norwegian society (Rugkåsa and Thorsen 2003). The work of Gullestad (1989, 1996), Eriksen (1993), Klausen (1984, 1992), Larsen (1984), Sørhaug (1984) and Vike (1997) are notable exceptions. Instead, the focus 'at home' was largely on minority groups viewed as the Other – such as the Sámi (Eidheim 1969, 1971; see also Vike, this volume), smaller-scale societies such as fishing communities and studies of migrants. Research on migration to a certain degree reflected heated public debates in Norway, with a focus on forced marriage, honour killing, female genital mutilation and gang criminality (e.g. Borchgrevink 1997; Grønhaug 1997; Lien 2015; Talle 2007; Wikan 1995, 2002), and integration issues (e.g. Fuglerud and Engebrigtsen 2009; Lidén 2017; Rugkåsa 2012) but some also asked questions such as how debates about migrants should be studied as debates about Norwegians themselves (Gullestad 2002). Public debates in Norway on migration and migrants have displayed a classic anthropological dilemma: the possibility of anthropologists providing both an understanding of minorities, *and* a critique of their ways of being based on majority values – connoting both ethnocentrism and relativism.

'Norwegianness' was often (and still is) presented in public debate as springing from a monolithic, liberal-egalitarian society with universal morality. Conversely, in studies of the Sámi, the idea of Norwegianness was barely expressed (Eriksen 2009). However, more recently, anthropologists have conducted systematic studies of the so-called majority population. These include comparative perspectives on the question of how Norway (or Scandinavia more widely) can be understood as a distinctive cultural region (Bendixsen *et al.* 2017), on what separates this region from the 'Western' world at large and why such peculiarities manifest themselves. The earlier observation by Marianne Gullestad (1992) that there is a Norwegian ethos of egalitarianism which depends on sameness is still used and modified (Lien *et al.* 2001). In studies of the rural socio-cultural landscape, its peculiar form of modernity and its conditions for development we may find continuities with Barth's interpretations of entrepreneurship (e.g. Barth 1967a, 1967b) in which the sphere concept is central (Bringslid 2012). Understandings of kinship – traditionally one of the key topics of anthropology – has also been pursued in research in the domestic site of the Norwegian anthropologists (Howell and Melhuus 2001; Lien and Abram 2019).

This described diversity in anthropological research 'at home' brings along different ethical and political challenges and methodological implications, makes use of very different theoretical and analytical perspectives and has different comparative aims. Where the Sámi represent the Fourth World (relating to academic and political discourses of and on indigenous peoples), immigrants have largely come to represent the Third World, the world's oppressed (Eriksen 2009). Another object of recent anthropological study, the Atlantic salmon, now so thoroughly domesticated in Norway (Lien 2015), represents a different ontological world altogether. The relation between researcher and object has become different and diverse, which suggests that the idea of fieldwork 'at home' should be dissolved since the term makes little sense.

Conclusion

I would like to return in the end to the mystery: How has this peculiar community, Norway's anthropologists, managed not only to survive but also to flourish in a time of economic crisis and intensified neoliberal audit culture? The first obvious point is that the Norwegian economy, and as a consequence, funding for research and higher education, has not really been struck that much by the global crisis. While anthropology departments do work under rather tight financial conditions, anthropologists in Norway have retained relative freedom to plan and carry out their research. The drive for market-oriented university research and the incorporation of public–private partnerships is surely present in Norway, but has developed more slowly than elsewhere.

In addition, I would reiterate that Norway has a significant density of anthropological engagement in media, public events and arenas of policy (Bringa and Bendixsen 2016). The continuous initiation of students into the sphere of anthropology contributes to the perspectives of anthropology being continuously recognized and valued in widening circles. The discipline's perceived social 'relevance' might also be enhanced by all the research actually carried out by anthropologists throughout Norway (Rugkåsa and Thorsen 2003).

The continued methodological commitment to in-depth research through long-term fieldwork, with a focus on current concerns and challenges of global significance, also means that anthropology remains a distinct discipline in Norway – it is not sociology, not cultural studies, not 'ethnography' seen purely as method. Perhaps one of the most important contributions of anthropology in Norway to anthropology as a discipline is the deep and enduring methodological dedication to fieldwork.

Anthropologists in Norway quite regularly suggest that there is a crisis in and for the discipline, or even that doomsday – the end of long-term fieldwork – is approaching, and that the terms and times of anthropology are indeed a-changing. However, compared to their peer communities abroad, the Norwegians still have plenty of space to pursue in-depth fieldwork and engage in anthropological knowledge formation in academia and beyond.

Acknowledgements

I would like to thank Edvard Hviding for discussions of several aspects of and directions taken by anthropology in Norway. His deep insights into the processes discussed in this chapter have been invaluable. Needless to say, I remain responsible for any mistakes and interpretations.

References

Argyrou, V. 2000. 'Self-accountability, ethics and the problem of meaning'. In M. Strathern (ed.), *Audit Cultures: Anthropological Studies in Accountability, Ethics and the Academy*, pp.196–212. London: Routledge.

Barth, F. 1967a. 'Economic spheres in Darfur'. In R. Firth (ed.), *Themes in Economic Anthropology*, pp. 149–74. London: Tavistock Publications.

——— (ed.). 1967b. *The Role of the Entrepreneur in Social Change in Northern Norway*. Oslo: Universitetsforlaget.

Bendixsen, S., Bringslid, M.B. and Vike H. (eds). 2017. *Egalitarianism in Scandinavia: Historical and Contemporary Approaches*. New York: Palgrave.

Bertelsen, B.E. 2012. 'Moving at the margins to re-centre anthropology: interview with Bruce Kapferer'. *Norsk Antropologisk Tidsskrift* 23(2):182–97.

Borchgrevink, T. 1997. 'Et ubehag i antropologien' [A discomfort in anthropology]. *Norsk Antropologisk Tidsskrift* 8(1):26–36.

Bringa, T. and Bendixsen, S. (eds). 2016. *Engaged Anthropology: Views from Scandinavia*. New York: Palgrave.

Bringslid, M.B. (ed.). 2012. *Bygdeutviklingas paradoks* [The paradox of rural development]. Oslo: Scandinavian Academic Press.

Eidheim, H. 1969. 'When ethnic identity is a social stigma'. In F. Barth (ed.), *Ethnic Groups and Boundaries: The Social organization of Culture Difference*, pp. 281–97. Oslo: Universitetsforlaget.

——— 1971. 'Lappish guest relationships under conditions of cultural change'. In H. Eidheim, *Aspects of the Lappish minority situation*, pp. 25–36. Oslo: Universitetsforlaget

Eriksen, T.H. 1993. 'Being Norwegian in a shrinking world: reflections on Norwegian identity'. In A.C. Kiel (ed.), *Continuity and Change: Aspects of Modern Norway*, pp. 11–38. Oslo: Scandinavian University Press.

———— 2009. 'Norwegian anthropologists study minorities at home: political and
      academic agendas'. *Anthropology in Action* 16(2):27–38.

———— 2015. *Fredrik Barth: An Intellectual Biography*. London: Pluto Press.

Fuglerud, Ø. and Engebrigtsen, A. 2009. *Kultur og generasjon: tilpasningsprosesser
      blant somaliere og tamiler i Norge* [Culture and generation: adaptation
      processes among Somalis and Tamils in Norway]. Oslo: Universitetsforlaget.

Goffman, E. 1959. *The Presentation of Self in Everyday Life*. New York: Anchor Books.

Grønhaug, R. 1997. 'Rettsstaten, det flerkulturelle og antropologien' [The rule of law,
      multiculturalism and anthropology]. *Norsk Antropologisk Tidsskrift* 3/4:
      267–77.

Gullestad, M. 1989. 'Small facts and large issues: the anthropology of contemporary
      Scandinavian society'. *Annual Review of Anthropology* 18:71–93.

———— 1992. *The Art of Social Relations: Essays on Culture, Social Action and
      Everyday Life in Modern Norway*. Oslo: Scandinavian University Press.

———— 1996. *Everyday Life Philosophers: Modernity, Morality, and Autobiography in
      Norway*. Oslo: Scandinavian University Press.

———— 2002. *Det Norske Sett med Nye Øyne: Kritisk Analyse av Norsk Innvandrings-
      debatt* [Norwegianness from a new perspective: critical analysis of the
      Norwegian immigration debate]. Oslo: Universitetsforlaget.

Harvey, P., Krohn-Hansen, C. and Nustad, K. (eds). 2019. *Anthropos and the Material*.
      Durham, NC: Duke University Press.

Hastrup, K., Garsten, C., Hansen, T.B., Mitchell, J.P. and Vuorela, U.M. 2011. 'Social
      and cultural anthropological research in Norway: an evaluation'. Oslo:
      Research Council of Norway, Division of Science.

Howell, S. and Melhuus, M. (eds). 2001. *Blod, tykkere enn vann? Betydninger av
      slektskap i Norge* [Blood, thicker than water? Meanings of kinship in
      Norway]. Bergen: Fagbokforlaget.

Klausen, A.M. 1992. 'Norsk kultur: myte eller realitet' [Norwegian culture: myth or
      reality]. In A.M. Klausen (ed.), *Kultur: Mønster og Kaos* [Culture: pattern
      and chaos], pp. 204–21. Oslo: Ad Notam Gyldendal.

———— (ed.). 1984. *Den Norske Væremåten* [Being Norwegian]. Oslo: J.W. Cappelens
      Forlag.

Larsen, T. 1984. 'Bønder i byen: på jakt etter den norske konfigurasjonen' [Peasants in
      the city: hunting for the Norwegian configuration]. In A.M. Klausen (ed.),
      Den Norske Væremåten [Being Norwegian], pp. 15–44. Oslo: J.W. Cappelens
      Forlag.

Lidén, H. 2017. *Barn og migrasjon: mobilitet og tilhørighet* [Children and migration:
      mobility and belonging]. Oslo: Universitetsforlaget.

Lien, M.E. 2015. *Becoming Salmon: Aquaculture and the Domestication of a Fish*.
      Berkeley: University of California Press.

Lien, M. and Abram, S. 2019. *Hytta: Fire vegger rundt en drøm* [The Cottage: Four walls around a dream]. Tanum: Oslo

Lien, M., Lidén, H. and Vike, H. (eds). 2001. *Likhetens Paradokser: Antropologiske Undersøkelser i det Moderne Norge* [Paradoxes of equality: anthropological investigations in modern Norway] Oslo: Universitetsforlaget.

Rugkåsa, M. 2012. *Likhetens Dilemma: om Sivilisering og Integrasjon i den Velferdsambisiøse Norske Stat* [The dilemma of equality: on civilizing and integration in Norway's welfare-ambitious state]. Oslo: Gyldendal Akademisk.

Rugkåsa, M. and Thorsen, K.T. 2003. *Nære Steder, Nye Rom: Utfordringer i Antropologiske Studier i Norge* [Nearby places, new spaces: challenges to anthropological studies in Norway]. Oslo: Gyldendal Akademisk.

Sørhaug, H.C. 1984. 'Totemisme på norsk: betraktninger om den norske sosialdemokratismens vesen' [Totemism, Norwegian style: reflections on the nature of Norwegian social democracy]. In A.M. Klausen (ed.), *Den Norske Væremåten* [Being Norwegian], pp. 61–87. Oslo: J.W. Cappelens Forlag.

Strathern, M. 2000. 'Introduction: new accountabilities'. In M. Strathern (ed.), *Audit Cultures: Anthropological Studies in Accountability, Ethics and the Academy*, pp. 1–18. London: Routledge.

Talle, A. 2007. *Om Kvinneleg Omskjering* [About Female Genital Mutilation]. Oslo: Samlaget.

Vike, H. 1997. 'Norsk kultur: myte og realitet' [Norwegian culture: myth and reality']. In T.H. Eriksen (ed.), *Flerkulturell Forståelse* [Multicultural understanding], pp. 122–38. Oslo: Tano Aschehoug.

——— 2018. *Politics and Bureaucracy in the Norwegian Welfare State*. New York: Palgrave.

Wikan, U. 1995. *Mot en Ny Norsk Underklasse: Innvandrere, Kultur og Integrasjon* [Towards a new Norwegian underclass: immigrants, culture and integration]. Oslo: Gyldendal Norsk Forlag.

——— 2002. *Generous Betrayal: Politics of Culture in the New Europe*. Chicago: University of Chicago Press.

8

Norwegian Anthropology Day

Panel discussion

✦

Editors' introduction

Social anthropology at its best is a discipline grounded in dialogue. From the outset, the vision of the Norwegian Anthropology Day was for its final part to be a wide-ranging panel discussion. A panel was recruited, with participants from all four Norwegian anthropology departments, and representatives also of doctoral and master's students, in addition to invited colleagues from British anthropology. Each invited panellist was given the floor for five to seven minutes. After they had all spoken, the two moderators helped facilitate a wide-ranging dialogue among the panel and with the audience. The following is an edited transcript from a sound recording of the panel presentations and subsequent discussion.

Most of the panellists in fact devised part of their interventions on the spot, as direct commentary on the presentations given earlier in the day. While the speakers were given opportunity in the editorial process to suggest minor revisions to their own contributions, the end result remains very close to the tone of the day and to the spoken, sometimes spontaneous and improvised, dialogue.

For some of our non-Norwegian colleagues, the informality and sometimes cheerful banter of the following pages may seem to be somewhat out of the ordinary and perhaps overly imprecise. But such is the nature of our eternal, internal conversations! As organizers of the Norwegian Anthropology Day and editors of this volume, we are very pleased to offer you this (lightly) edited transcription, so true to the spirit of the day.

The panellists must be commended for their ability to speak so eloquently and spontaneously on the issues raised during the Norwegian Anthropology Day, and for their stamina in continuing lively discussion for three hours, interrupted only by a brief tea and coffee break.

As chair of the Norwegian Anthropology Day, one of us introduced the two moderators – professors Annelin Eriksen and Christine M. Jacobsen, both of the University of Bergen – and the nine panellists[1] then spoke in the sequence announced in advance, before discussion was opened to the floor.

Discussion

EDVARD HVIDING: And now, the panel, to be moderated by two of my favourite Norwegian anthropologists. One is Professor Annelin Eriksen, the vice-dean for research at our Faculty of Social Sciences.[2] She was once my student; now she is my boss. Annelin is known for exercising discipline when running classes and collective events such as this one. The same applies to Professor Christine Jacobsen, by her side. Annelin and Christine are also close friends: sometimes we don't know who is speaking, because their dialects are only slightly different! Christine is professor and director of the Centre for Women's and Gender Research at the University of Bergen, and as such one of the key anthropologists beyond our Bergen department. And here is the panel, nine fine anthropologists altogether. I now leave the rest to you, and please remember that Annelin and Christine are strict seminar leaders who keep time!

CHRISTINE M. JACOBSEN: Thank you for this introduction, Edvard, and welcome. We're delighted to moderate this truly classic panel – in fact I think it is the largest panel I have ever chaired. We shall have a very interesting and lively debate. We have persons representing all the large teaching and research institutions in anthropology in Norway. We have researchers in different stages of their careers: from master's students to PhD candidates, all the way to very experienced professors. Together they represent the breadth and width of Norwegian anthropology. We know that you will engage with us in discussion among these fantastic anthropologists. We also have some of our British colleagues in the panel, and they are especially welcome.

ANNELIN ERIKSEN: The way we will organize this is that each of panel member will be given five to seven minutes. And we will be strict on timekeeping, as

---

1   Two of the invited panellists originally listed were unable to participate.
2   Subsequent to the Norwegian Anthropology Day, Annelin Eriksen became the University of Bergen's vice-rector for global relations from 2017 to 2021.

there are so many of you. Your allocated time will partly be used to reflect on the presentations we heard before lunch, although each of you also has a predetermined role, so to speak. When we have all finished there will be a short break, after which we will come back into this room to engage with the audience with any comments and questions they might have.

CHRISTINE M. JACOBSEN: Since we Norwegians very much appreciate our 'Norway friends' – this being our vernacular term for famous people who come to us and decide to keep on visiting because we are such likeable people – we will first give the floor to a true 'Norway friend': Professor Penny Harvey from the University of Manchester.

PENNY HARVEY: Well, thank you very much! Thank you to the RAI and to Edvard and Synnøve. It's a bit embarrassing, really, to be the first one out here. I think the excuse is probably that I did become a 'Norway friend' when I first had the fantastic good luck to begin a Professor II position for a couple of years in Bergen.[3] I enjoyed it so much and have had amazing fortune to be able to repeat the experience in Oslo. I truly value the time that I have spent in these two anthropology departments, and it's a real honour to be able to comment today.

I've been thinking: What is it then that is specific about Norwegian anthropology? Let me run past you the idea that maybe it's about a very particular form of determined internationalism. It may be because of the particular position that I have in the Norwegian academy, but I have always been struck by the constant stream of visitors that come through the Norwegian anthropology departments. And it is not just the Professor IIs. For every PhD defence there are two external examiners, and often these are two international colleagues. Post-doctoral positions are often taken up by non-Norwegians, and like anywhere else in the world, the PhD students come from far and wide. Everyone is doing ethnography, and in all parts of the world. Many Norwegian anthropologists are trained outside Norway, and it seems that everyone is travelling all the time. The departments therefore feel

---

3   At universities in Norway, a Professor II is someone who is a professor at another institution, at home or abroad, who is recruited to work in a department or research centre for specific strategic reasons, such as for building a research or teaching portfolio that is weak or absent, or for further augmenting or strengthening an already established research group. A Professor II receives 20 per cent of the annual professorial salary and is duly expected to contribute this proportion of work in addition to their existing position. A Professor II is usually appointed on a fixed-term contract of three or four years, which may be renewed.

incredibly international and there is a real ethos of international engagement. And last but not least, I think that it's really important to note that Norwegian anthropologists routinely work in English. Everyone is expected to not just speak and read English, but to write and publish in English. So think about what that means by comparison to working in England: if we all had to do all our work in another language we'd probably grind to a halt!

And then I wondered whether it is a paradox to say that determined internationalism makes for a distinctly Norwegian anthropology. I think that there is a case for that point of view when we think of some of the talks this morning on the history of Norway's international engagement. One important contrast with the British context is that this history is not overwhelmed by the legacy of colonial engagement, which makes a significant difference to the sensibilities that emerge in and around ethnographic work.

But then there is something particular to fill out in terms of Norwegian political and economic history, which has only been mentioned in passing today. I'm referring to the oil boom that has shaped contemporary Norway and its place on the international stage. It is worth reflecting on how oil money has been spent in Norway. I am particularly interested in infrastructure, and have been amazed at the infrastructural provision afforded to small remote communities who not only have well-maintained roads but also benefit from tunnels to shorten routes and improve connectivity. The oil money has been invested to create an integrated national territory, but it also provokes anthropologists to take up critical projects and to show concern over extractive projects in the Arctic, over the environmental effects of fossil fuels, and the effects of oil on international markets, and on international relations more generally. I think that's very distinctive. But so is the way in which the oil money was invested in relations, in persons and in institutions at home. We have been joking about how, in Norway, international programme reviews are followed up with supportive funding. That is no small thing. In many other places in the world, such reviews are instead used to justify funding cuts, and I think that also makes a real difference to the horizons of Norwegian anthropology.

A related point I wanted to elaborate on is the place of PhD students in Norway's anthropology departments. They are employed as salaried members of staff, and in that sense are truly integral to the departments, with equal voice on the departmental boards. This arrangement affected me directly as it was Cecilie Ødegaard who initiated my Professor II position in Bergen. She needed a PhD supervisor; there wasn't anybody around in the department who could supervise on Latin America at the time, so they brought in someone from abroad to do it. The other thing that I think is remarkable about Norwegian PhD experience is the doctoral defence. If you've ever had the luck to be an

examiner for a PhD in Norway, you will be familiar with the elaborate ritual. It
is in fact a ritual of accomplishment that I would really like to see in the UK,
but we don't do it like that. We shut the candidate in a room with two grumpy
professors, and by the end of the examination the candidate is sometimes not
even sure if they have passed or not – that was my personal experience! But
in Norway, the candidates are required to publicly perform their new-found
status as professional anthropologists. They deliver a lecture, and they engage
in public debate with two esteemed examiners in the presence of colleagues,
family and friends. The work is thus presented in public, and the achievement
of the PhD is acknowledged in the presentation of the candidate as a scholar.
But things don't end there. After the official part there is usually a really
amazing party, which the candidate often puts on at great expense. They invite
their family, their peer group, their supervisors, their examiners. They make
speeches, they eat, they drink, they dance. And they basically acknowledge
that to produce anthropology is to be part of a community of scholars and of
a wider support network. This is the kind of ecosystem of intellectual life that
I think is made very explicit in Norway.

Of course, there are times when I think that Norwegian anthropology
settles into a specificity from which you can feel excluded. Sometimes, and
quite rightly, they may start doing their 'real' business in Norwegian. And
publishing in Norwegian is of distinct value. There are national conferences,
where in some contexts you might be expected to speak Norwegian. Finally,
when you get a permanent post – unlike the position of Professor II – you
are expected to learn Norwegian. This is all part and parcel of how the
departments really do conduct their business in a seriously egalitarian way.

So that whole way in which Norwegian anthropologists move between
English and Norwegian is really interesting and reinforces my claim that
Norwegian anthropology is a very international discipline; but even so, we've
still got what Synnøve mentioned in her talk (Bendixsen, this volume), that
funding agencies actually complain that Norwegians don't have sufficient
visibility internationally! This, I think, to be honest, is just part and parcel
of the paradigm of how the evaluations are carried out: you cut Norwegian
anthropology out of its circuits of relations, and you evaluate it in isolation,
instead of drawing attention to the fundamental contributions made to the
building of international networks. Evaluators may say, 'Hey, no international
network here'. Well, they've just severed it. These modes of evaluation –
probably imported from the UK – attribute value only in terms of winners
and losers. International evaluation requires you to be world leading – if you
are not 'first' then somehow you don't exist. But what world would we be in
if everyone was out in front? It would not be a real world, it would not be the

world that gets celebrated when the PhD students perform their expertise *and* produce their networks for all to see in the context of the public defence.

I think that in some sense it's not really that the international profile of Norwegian anthropology is weak. It's that the evaluation process systematically erases the international profile from view. I would like to suggest another image that I might leave you with. There's been some discussion this morning about how Norwegian anthropology is somehow marginal. And I want to ask whether Norway is actually on the margin. I think in terms of a parallel from Latin America. In Amazonia there are so-called 'marginal' groups who know themselves to be at the centre of the world; they may be the centre not just of the world, but of the universe. There are also arguments from the anthropology of the state that the margins are in fact constitutive of the centre, and that the centre does not exist without the margins.

I once remarked to a colleague that maybe the Norwegians bring all these anthropologists from all over the world to be part of their conversations because they feel they are on the margins. And my colleague said: 'No they don't, they just go, "Come here and talk to us".' And I think there is a truth to that. I'll leave you just with that image: When David Harvey[4] came to Manchester, I had to sit in a room with a thousand people in order to listen to him. When David Harvey came to Bergen, we had a private audience. There were twelve of us who sat and had lunch with him. I think that, in Norway, you bring people in mostly on your own terms. I've had the opportunity to meet some of the most renowned anthropologists in the world in Norway, but not to the same extent in Britain. I'll leave you with that. By building an international community, Norwegian anthropology defies the very notion of marginality.

UNNI WIKAN: Thank you for inviting me to contribute to this very special occasion. I regret that I have not been able to prepare my comments beforehand, so I must make them up on the spot. But I have listened attentively and taken notes during the presentations, and I will make some comments based on that.

To the question 'Is there a Norwegian anthropology?' my answer is 'No.' My assessment is inevitably affected by my own position, my mentors and my career. I have been with both the Bergen and the Oslo departments of social anthropology, as well as the Ethnographic Museum at the University of Oslo.

---

4   David Harvey is an internationally renowned Marxist geographer and social theorist, Distinguished Professor of Anthropology & Geography at the Graduate Center of the City University of New York (CUNY), and the Director of Research at the Center for Place, Culture and Politics. See davidharvey.org.

I was a student in Bergen, an associate professor at the Ethnographic Museum and a professor first there, then at the Oslo department, which joined with the museum in 1987 under one umbrella. They split again around the millennium and I moved back to the department, in 2002.

In my experience, Norwegian anthropology is a mixture of things: approaches, perspectives, theoretical views. There is not *a* Norwegian anthropology, but several *anthropologies*, and they seem to have grown over the years. On visits to various foreign departments, on the other hand, I encounter the idea that there *is* a Norwegian anthropology. I think this is due to a perception that anthropology in a small country like Norway bears the mark of some distinctive figures, and that we are collectively shaped by a very strong fieldwork ethic and a down-to-earth approach, rather than drawn to desk work and high-flown theory. I think there is something to this: there is a *grounding* to Norwegian anthropology that is special, and that we are proud to share.

But I also think that seen from within, the *differences* in doing anthropology in Norway are striking – leading me to answer the question 'Is there a Norwegian anthropology?' in the negative: I don't like the plural *anthropologies*, which I just used about the Norwegian scene – it is trendy and unclear. But it evokes what I really want to underscore: that Norwegian anthropology is a composite of very many different approaches and perspectives. This pertains both to theory and method. The differences go back in time, at least to the Marxist battles in the late 1960s, and they are constantly being nurtured by various developments, among them the hiring of faculty members with limited knowledge of Norwegian traditions of knowledge and language. Penny [Harvey] said that foreign faculty were obliged to learn to teach in Norwegian within a certain time, but the rule was never applied and seems to have been abandoned, at least in Oslo. With the sheer numbers and diversity of people doing anthropology in various capacities in Norway nowadays and the ease of international communication, a distinct *Norwegian* anthropology is not what I see.

But we Norwegians are proud of our fieldwork traditions, and here there *is* some common ground. I think we all agree that good fieldwork is essential for good anthropology, but I also think we need to ask: What do we actually mean by fieldwork? There are many different conceptions around. I have had close contact with anthropology in the United States throughout my career, and over there everybody is 'doing ethnography' nowadays. It's the big thing, the 'real' thing, the mark of engagement with real events. We anthropologists are also doing ethnography, but what is it about *our* engagement and *our* kind of fieldwork that is distinctive to our form of social anthropology? *Is* there something we can spell out? I think we need a discussion about that, and not just to celebrate how good we Norwegians are when it comes to fieldwork. We need some critique to help us see better what are the prospects and pitfalls on the road ahead.

When I was a student in Bergen, what attracted me to social anthropology and kept me there was its engagement with real persons, real lives and social process in a comparative perspective. I was interested in lived experience across cultures and what shaped it. I have been sorry to see over the years that what might now be called a person-centred anthropology is hardly taught in anthropology in Norway. Much of anthropology today, in my view, is not about people or persons but about 'big issues', and especially trendy issues, because that's where the money lies. Anthropology in the past – and for some of us to this day – was an inexpensive venture. It didn't cost much to do fieldwork. Anthropology today is about money and big money. It marks the whole discipline, also in little Norway. It shapes *what* anthropologists do, *how* they do it, and *why* – for better and worse. What's the impact on a presumed Norwegian anthropology?

The Oslo department, the one I have known best, has undergone a marked change in the composition of its faculty over the past ten years. Broad regional coverage is dwindling, and female to male membership is reduced from near equality (or a slight female majority) to just a quarter compared to men at present. It has all happened in the name of hiring the best applicant to vacant positions. But as all of us know, 'the best' is rarely just best. There are considerations and preferences of various kinds at work. An anthropological analysis of what is actually going on would be interesting. From my perspective, it is untenable for an anthropology department to let its regional coverage diminish as much as Oslo has done. It is well and good to have solid regional coverage of a few parts of the world and to say that regions do not matter, it is the thematic and project proposals and theories we develop that really count. I think this is too simple. I think we really do need much better and broader regional expertise to challenge much of what we think we know and to give the students a better grounding in cultural comparison. I think both this, and hiring more women, can be done without sacrificing our shared endeavour to get *the best.*

Now to theory. I'm very critical of the evaluation of Norwegian anthropology (Hastrup *et.al.* 2011) that concluded that we're not doing enough theory.[5] I think it reflects a misconception both about what Norwegian anthropology is, and what theory is, and a misguided separation of the two.

---

5   The reference is to the international evaluation of anthropological research at Norwegian universities and institutes carried out during 2009–10, commissioned by the Research Council of Norway.

Theory and method are linked. Given the strong grounding of anthropology in Norway on fieldwork, theory moves rather close to the ground, for most of us. It is not hovering 'up there'. It does not take flight and become delinked from the empirical evidence in a loftier language. It is embedded. Perhaps there *is* a Norwegian anthropology in this sense, after all? We never stop building and using theory.

Now, the really good thing about Norwegian anthropology is that we have fabulous opportunities for fieldwork. In no other country that I know do colleagues have similar opportunities. We're envied all over the place. The whole ethos of Norwegian anthropology is that the more fieldwork, the better, and departments move on that score. Teaching can often be concentrated to parts of the semester to allow *some* time for fieldwork, and other options, like 'buying' free time may also be possible. We have relatively good funding, and some of us still don't need much for the way we work. When all is said and done I think it is *this* that might be the crux of Norwegian anthropology and gives us a shared sense of identity: fieldwork is our temple. Whether we go there or not, it is what we believe in and what keeps us on our paths, however much we diverge in anthropological practice. The centre holds.

Sidsel Saugestad: I will give some reflections from the perspective of what is now the Arctic University of Norway, established in Tromsø in the 1970s as a new university *in* and *for* the north. In the early years, it was very fruitful to combine teaching and research that addressed Sámi issues and Sámi–Norwegian relations, and use some of the key achievements in Norwegian anthropology to focus exactly on these topics. Our friend Thomas [Hylland Eriksen] has observed that the department in Bergen was established on 'Barth 1966', *Models of Social Organization*, whereas the department in Tromsø was established on the basis of 'Barth 1969', *Ethnic Groups and Boundaries*. Indeed, that little book was tremendously important both in terms of material, perspective and approach, ready to use for analysis on situations in northern Norway, or northern Scandinavia more broadly.

I have two reflections about how this developed, which are more on the concept on *engaged* anthropology than on Norwegian anthropology as such. First, from the very beginning of the Tromsø anthropology department, then called Sámi studies, the people who were the topic of research were also present in the classroom. So the idea about 'the native speaks back', which appeared as somewhat new in the anthropology literature of the 1980s, was in fact an element in our teaching from the very start. It caused both enthusiasm and antagonism. But it was all very, very engaged, as we were exposed to events which changed both the Norwegian political landscape and the relationship between the Norwegian state and the Sámi, as Olaf [Smedal] discussed in his talk today (see Smedal, this volume).

My second point is that following from this situation, the study of ethnic groups developed into a more specialized strand of anthropological research in Norway: the study of and engagement with the emerging international movement of indigenous peoples – part of the reason for this being that the Sámi were very active in this global process.

The closeness to these events and processes had many consequences. One was the need to be more explicit in the ethical aspects of the relationships between the researcher and the group being researched. This applies especially to indigenous peoples worldwide, who are in particularly vulnerable situations. At our university we developed a model for this – an ideal to move from research *on* Sámi/indigenous peoples (the standard colonial asymmetrical relationship) to research *with* them, meaning capacity-building, scholarships and teaching, and ultimately to research *by* them – an ideal situation where no one group has a monopoly, but all have the same tools for analysing the situations at hand.

Gunnar [Sørbø] described some quite similar strategies, using different words, in his account of collaborations with the University of Khartoum (see Sørbø, this volume). Some of us in Tromsø had the opportunity later to try out our model in a Southern African setting, developing a research agenda aiming to do away with research *on* the exotic, photogenic San (Bushmen) to involving them in research *with* them, gradually trying to give more of them the capacity and competence to do research on their own situation. I'm not saying this to make a very original point, but just to exemplify a possible approach to the practicalities of setting up structures to engage on more equal terms with the people we do research on.

MARTIN THOMASSEN: It may seem that in Norway we seem to have quite a homogeneous orientation in the discipline. We have rather few anthropological sub-disciplines. This is what I want to engage you in, based on my experiences in my department in Trondheim, which is a bit odd within social anthropology in Norway. Odd in a very positive way, I would add. Unni [Wikan] problematized this in terms of how distinctive Norwegian anthropology is. There may be some disagreement on variations here, and as for me I do think there are different anthropologies in Norway, but I don't want to exaggerate this too much.

But let us follow up on this point and note that the mindset in Norway invariably is to think in terms of centre/periphery. And in relation to Bergen and Oslo, we in Trondheim are at the margin, the periphery. Let me continue along that track and note that, yes, Norwegian anthropology overall shows a homogeneous orientation at the national level. But that being so, maybe variations and exceptions are all the more interesting.

My department is actually celebrating its fortieth anniversary this year [2015]. Its founding father was Jan Brøgger, a psychologist who engaged in anthropology, and who joined together the best of what he understood as anthropology and psychology. If we say that Tromsø started as more like a political project, I guess the project that set us off in Trondheim would be the concerns about the alienation of individuals, borrowing the best from Erving Goffman's theories of roles and impression management, and picking up some terms from Freud such as repression and anxiety. That would be the starting point of social anthropology in Trondheim.

Now, in the 1970s, Brøgger was an excellent promoter of the public understanding of anthropology. He wrote popular books and contributed articles to newspapers pretty much on a weekly basis. And he engaged an entire region of Norway, continuously, by writing about matters that actually were on everybody's tongue at any given point in time. In that sense Brøgger's intervention in the world came from a wish to make a difference based on marrying psychology and anthropology. That he was an excellent spokesman for his ambition did not mean that people agreed with him, however. In fact, many anthropologists around Norway disagreed with him, but no one could say that he was not a fine intellectual and an inspiring and engaging actor in public debate.

Brøgger established an anthropology department in a city that already had (and even more so now) a very large sector of applied research institutes engaged with technology, industry and studies of work and labour conditions. As he moved around in elite circles, at one point some industrialists offered us a professorship in 'organizational anthropology'. And if you look at the department's portfolio today, perhaps the majority of our PhD students are engaged in organizational anthropology in one way or another. Upon completing their PhDs, they tend to take up jobs in one of Trondheim's applied research institutes, especially in jobs broadly concerned with studies of work.

NTNU, the Norwegian University of Science and Technology, at which our department is located, is itself a little bit odd, because not only is it large, but it caters to the training of what I might call 'social engineers'. And so one of the things that our research and (particularly) teaching are geared towards is to train 'social engineering' students to think about technology by using Mauss, seeing technology as a 'total social fact'. I would like to think of our department as making a positive contribution to the anthropology of knowledge, particularly by focusing on the relationship between knowledge and technology.

We look critically at the 'technologification' of knowledge, through which, from a widespread point of view, knowledge that cannot be turned into technology does not count. Another variation would be to consider the 'entification' of knowledge, in which knowledge not entitively quantified or measured does not count. This relates to what Thomas [Hylland Eriksen] talked about when he used the word 'prevailing knowledge regime'. In Trondheim, we are engaged in critically studying prevailing knowledge regimes, looking at the particular relationships between knowledge and technology, and in fact we have a major research project about that right now called 'The cultural logic of facts and figures'.[6]

MARIT MELHUUS: I would really like to thank the RAI and the organizers. It is such a privilege to be here today with you all. I have a couple of points I want to make first. We heard this morning about some particularities, if not peculiarities, of Norwegian anthropology and how they have developed over time; we heard about our history, the role of fieldwork, public engagement and north–south relations. I shall be spending my allocated few minutes to say something about how these histories have translated into certain patterns and variations. I will focus on the departments in Oslo and Bergen.

Let us assume that there is a tradition of what we call 'generalist anthropology'. This is, of course, not unique to Norway. However, the prevailing attitude here has been a significant reluctance to accept any kind of hyphenated category of anthropology as a way of classifying – or structuring – what we do. We don't do the anthropology of war, or the anthropology of religion, and so forth. We claim to be generalist in our orientation. The only distinction, I will claim (and my colleagues might not agree), is that there has always been a propensity towards 'regional specialization', independent of whether or not regions are something that are considered to exist. We still hold that broad regional expertise is important to the overall profile of the department, as it is also important to anthropology. Both generalist ideology and regional specialization, then, have concrete ramifications and spill over into how we go about organizing our departments in terms of teaching and recruitment. What are those ramifications? Let me examine the regional one first.

Basically, we always hire the best candidate for a vacant position, irrespective of regional specialization. Only rarely do we specify that we wish our potential new colleague to be specialized in one particular region. But despite this, I believe, the regional component is always one dimension that is considered in hiring, and we continue to be concerned about the regional

6   See this project's website: www.ntnu.edu/sosant/cuff (accessed 20 June 2020).

composition of the department. If there are too many (or enough) Latin Americanists in our department, chances are the next person hired will not be a Latin Americanist. This might be totally irrespective of the theoretical or thematic approach of the persons to be considered. So already at this point we encounter problems regarding the kinds of themes we want and which regions we want present. Moreover, we know that in the course of a career, anthropologists might change their regions, their themes, their theoretical perspectives, so there should really not be any good reason to hire on the basis of regional specialization.

The generalist ideology is also implied in our consistent ambition to hire 'the best candidate'. Yet, and this connects to what Synnøve [Bendixsen] said, whoever is hired is expected to teach any course at the undergraduate level, and although in practice teaching is distributed in such a way that courses may be assigned to perhaps match some underlying interests that the teacher might have, in theory the expectation is that 'anyone can do anything'. Or as we might say in Norway: We are potatoes and can be used for anything.

The idea of the generalist might also be one explanation for how we design a curriculum or syllabus. Within the bachelor's programme, some courses are mandatory and some are optional. For mandatory courses we have a fixed curriculum. For example, when revising our bachelor's programme just recently, we had several committees – each of three people, and I was on two of them – to revise the syllabuses of all mandatory courses. The assumption is not only that a new fixed syllabus, once set, will last for years and the job is therefore done, but also – and more importantly – that anyone among our staff should be able to teach that particular syllabus. This applies to all mandatory undergraduate courses.

One of our recently hired staff from the UK in fact commented on this 'very strange way of teaching', because he was being set to teach 'someone else's course', as he put it. He had to teach a course designed by someone else, but without really having access to the underlying ideas that shaped the course's particular reading list. It would seem that, intuitively, we should recognize the 'mastermind' that joined all the monographs and articles together, and we should know the reason for including one monograph and not another one.

I think this might be a particular Norwegian way of doing things: letting a certain collective spirit shape a course rather than leaving it to the individual teacher. This runs counter to any individualistic ideology. But this way of doing things also perhaps neglects another widely shared idea about the importance of the continued evolution of anthropological knowledge. The flipside is that you very rarely have the chance to give what was once rather tellingly described as *con amore* lectures, where the teacher was free to design the syllabus and could literally teach from the heart. That is almost impossible at our department now.

Moreover, the generalist approach has repercussions for supervision. As with teaching, it is assumed that anyone can supervise anyone at the undergraduate level. In practice there is an attempt to match student and supervisor with some overlap of interest and competence, but not necessarily. Insofar as our master's students are more or less free to choose any topic of interest for their thesis, we have no sanctions when it comes to supervision. Again, we aim to supervise 'anything' that is feasible within the framework of the MA degree. This also, in some ways, spills over to the PhD students, although at this level more effort is made to ensure that regional and thematic expertise needed to supervise a particular PhD student is available at the department. Or if not, perhaps the department might hire a Professor II, as we heard from Penny [Harvey], who was appointed in Bergen at a time when no expertise on Latin America was available there. A Professor II may of course also be hired to fill a thematic specialty.

In any case, the problem in the end is that despite all good ambitions and efforts concerning a generalist approach, when it comes down to the concrete workings of a department, the ambitions do create some dilemmas. It would be interesting to hear if this resonates with the rest of you.

TORD AUSTDAL:[7] First of all, I would like to thank you for the invitation to participate in this panel, and as a junior researcher at the PhD level I shall be humble and admit that I have learned a lot about the history of my own discipline today. It has introduced me to new facets of a history in which we have engaged collectively in Norway this last year, through the various celebrations of the Bergen department's own history. There is also an ongoing discussion in Norway on whether there in fact *is* a Norwegian anthropology, and Professor Wikan just said 'no'.

I'm not going to get into that debate much, but nevertheless, given how I here represent a fairly large group of PhD research fellows in Norway, I would like to add one thing that emerged through today's larger collective retrospection – and that is the somewhat privileged position of PhD candidates today, compared to earlier. For, when speaking to colleagues from other countries, the conversation eventually – indeed almost without exception – turns to funding. And I think this is one minor, but very important, way in which Norwegian academic life as well as today's Norwegian anthropology (for the time being at least) differs somewhat from other academic scenes.

---

7   Tord Austdal completed and received his PhD in 2016, and is now an associate
     professor in social science at the University of Stavanger.

I am of course referring to the way that early-career anthropologists embark on their doctoral training as actual employees of the department, as mentioned by Professor Harvey. I think it is also important to take into consideration the Norwegian ethic of actively incorporating PhD candidates as true employees in departments. There is perhaps a slight bias, since I cannot really speak about the experience of all PhD research fellows in Norway, but as for my time in Bergen, I note that the incorporation of both PhD and postdoctoral fellows, their integration into the everyday life of the department, is an articulated institutional strategy. And I know that there have been vicious fights fought on various fronts to keep our presence within the department, both physically and academically. But I think that these two issues of institutional incorporation and the privileged level of funding shapes the way in which being a PhD student in a department is a meaningful – yes, even lucrative – endeavour. I see this as an expression of an academic culture that is in some strange way perceived to be very Norwegian, in the sense of being egalitarian, in the process valuing the work that is done by PhD fellows who are then more than simply 'students'.

This leads me to my second point, which is also about how there are different categories of PhDs in the Norwegian system. We know that there is no longer an opportunity to apply to the Research Council of Norway for individual PhD projects. All PhDs funded by the research council now come as elements of larger projects under the leadership of a professor. Concurrently, departments need to secure funding from their university to maintain a minimum 'pool' of PhD fellowships for individuals, giving them the opportunity to develop a novel personal project that has no strings attached, as it were. Such PhDs are not channelled through a larger research project, but can be proposed without any prior affiliation. To conclude: there is a certain emerging diversity of PhD 'trajectories', in response to which the departments now, in light of these new funding patterns, need to actively maintain diversity to secure the continued thematic and regional specialization of each PhD project.

KAJA BERG HJUKSE:[8] I have been invited here on behalf of the master's students in Trondheim, Tromsø, Bergen and Oslo to talk about the experience of the Norwegian research-based master's programme. The master's thesis, around which the Norwegian degree is centred, is an independent piece of work based on personal investigation through fieldwork. In Oslo, where I am a student, we are expected to spend five to eight months on fieldwork and data collection.

---

8   Kaja Berg Hjukse completed her master's degree in 2016 and is now a PhD
     candidate in the Department of Social Anthropology, University of Oslo.

I will begin by shortly introducing my own project. I returned this summer [2015] from fieldwork on reproductive practices in Myanmar. The background for the project was to see birth as a site where women conceptualize and organize their social and cultural worlds. I conducted six months of fieldwork in a village in Myanmar. Most of the time I was based in a monastic clinic and followed the health workers there, as well as the local midwives, as they provided care for women during pregnancy and birth. I observed clinical encounters, even a home birth, and I am now in the process of describing and analysing this material for my thesis, in what I take to be a set of complex relationships between the individual and the state, and the state and civil society.

On average, about 30 per cent of the students in our department do fieldwork in Oslo or elsewhere in Norway. The rest of us travel abroad. One of my fellow students, for example, went to Buenos Aires to study conversion to Islam among Argentine women. Another fellow student stayed in Oslo, where she studied health and food habits in a public primary school. Previous experience, language skills and many coincidences create the routes we follow. In comparison to other master's programmes, I think we tend to be a very mature and adventurous group of students. Some of us have years of work experience – I myself took a year off working as a primary school teacher, and was therefore able to visit Myanmar twice, building a network and attending Burmese language classes in preparation for my study.

To be honest, ambition seems to be more or less a prerequisite for even entering the master's programme in anthropology. In addition to attending regular courses, we spend our first semester defining our research and preparing for fieldwork. This includes finding your research site, fixing your visa, searching for literature, developing the project draft in consultation with a supervisor and applying for funding support, as well as language preparations, if needed. It is overwhelming, and far too hectic!

Earlier this autumn, in September, I attended the annual cabin trip for the Oslo master's students. Some of those who had just returned from fieldwork were invited to share our experiences. It was striking how the stories were all so alike. We had all been in different locations and looked at very different things, but we shared similar experiences and insights. In addition to the existential crises and all the frustrations of fieldwork, we shared a renewed understanding and respect for our discipline. The most difficult part, however, is the one we are currently in: the transformation of field notes into data and analysis.

To have a research-based master's programme that requires fieldwork allows us to undertake a real research project in miniature. We learn the tools and the crafts of anthropological knowledge. This, I would argue, is important as it gives us a taste of what it would mean to continue within academia, and to fail and learn before doing so. We are taught that it is not the answers that we give but the questions that we ask at the end of our thesis that are the most important and the potential basis for a PhD.

For those who enter a career path outside academia, the research-based master's programme makes them more attractive in the labour market. What makes us stand out from the sociologists and students of cultural studies is the knowledge, the independence and the inquisitiveness that results from the experience of fieldwork and from the production of an anthropological text based on personal investigation.

JAN PETER LAURENS LOOVERS: I am speaking on behalf of the Aberdeen department.[9] Tim Ingold wanted to be here but was unable to attend, and since I have belonged to the same department as Ingold since 2004, they asked if I could go instead, and I was very happy to do so. My own history with Norwegian anthropology started in 2007 when I was member of a large collaborative project that brought together a lot of anthropologists from Scandinavia, the United States, Canada and South Africa. In 2009 I went to Tromsø for one semester. Coming back then to the UK, I work now with colleagues at Oslo and Tromsø.

I would like to start talking a little bit about what Sidsel [Saugestad] was referring to, because it comes close to my own experiences of Tromsø, and that's about the interplay between Sámi studies, the development of anthropology, and to some degree also visual studies. I found that especially in Tromsø there was a lot of freedom, and someone explained to me once (Sidsel might say whether it's true or not) that because Tromsø is so far north it is at the margins of Norwegian anthropology, which enables them to pursue deeply political activities and meetings. They have an annual conference where they bring together African spokespersons. At the same time, the university's Centre for Sámi studies is quite a wonderful institution.

So given this background, I have been thinking about similarities and differences between British and Norwegian anthropology, and I think that one obvious distinction is that in Norway there are indigenous people, but not in the UK. I am intrigued by how Norwegian anthropology has relations with the Sámi, but as we have heard at the same time there are also conflicts of interest.

I do think there is a Norwegian anthropology, and the reason is Fredrik Barth, who I think is the founding father. As an exercise of the imagination, I wonder what would be the difference in Norwegian anthropology without

---

9   Jan Peter Laurens Loovers is presently an exhibition curator at the British Museum.

Fredrik Barth. About public engagements: within departments of anthropology and in British universities in general as well, there is a lot of discussion about public engagement and how to increase it. My background is from the Netherlands, and I find that there, as well as in Norway, there is stronger public engagement – whereas this sort of dialogue in the UK is much less visible.

The final thing is the availability of funding. At the moment in Aberdeen we are facing cuts, and we are in the process of having difficult dialogues with the senior management. Now the oil that flows through Aberdeen as a European oil city does not flow through the anthropology department; neither does the University of Aberdeen principal find anthropology particularly important. Oil and gas – the money goes to oil and gas and the management says we need to sponsor energy and channel funds to our energy departments. So in terms of oil there seems to be another difference here, and I find it difficult to critique that particular side of Norwegian anthropology.

INGJERD HOËM: Thank you so much, and thanks, everybody, for being here and enduring what must be one of the largest panels ever! I would like to thank Penny Harvey especially, for reminding us that it's not only a matter of having money or having oil; it's a matter of what the money is used for, as also the last speaker said. It's a matter of public engagement and intellectual engagement, how that money is used, channelled – and I think what we've seen today is a relatively thriving anthropological community. That is because we have had so many people working for us in the departments to make this possible, but it's also something that can very easily be lost.

And that also goes for us in Norway. I think that what we need to be very mindful of is that the relationships that we have across the sea means that in Oslo we don't have to 'go to Bergen to go abroad', as Fredrik [Barth] and Edvard Hviding reminded us! Of course there has been a bit of competition between Bergen and Oslo: we've had the big founding fathers, Fredrik Barth in particular; we've in fact had such a large number of people who have worked, separately and in cooperation, to create Norwegian anthropology – over so many years. Then in the 1980s and particularly the 1990s we had a certain transformation that you've also experienced in Britain, I'm sure – sometime around then was when the period of the 'big men' ended. In fact, I've heard people of my generation – I was born in 1960 so that defines it – in Norway and in Britain, lamenting the fact that we do not have the 'big scholars' any more. Well, it is a matter of debate whether that is a blessing or something to lament, I would say. But let me just give you a brief impression as seen from Oslo.

I started my studies in the department at the end of the 1970s, and the discussions then were very, very heated. We disagreed a lot! It wasn't about just sort of letting a hundred flowers bloom. We were in fact chopping down flowers, and we were quite aggressive at times. I know that was also the fact in Britain, and perhaps to such a degree that people were at times quite scared of entering the public debate, especially in Britain, perhaps, since people here are so incredibly good at being vicious with words – at cutting people down verbally. Of course such aggression is also a way of furthering theory, and most certainly a method of theorizing which creates a lot of attention – but such approaches also make it difficult for younger scholars, not to say students, to enter into the kind of positions that the big men of the time created.

Nevertheless, we are all empiricists, as you have heard today, and as empiricists we also know how to *think* with ethnography. We know, or at least knew, how to develop our own thinking, which was our model for everyone and every purpose, I think. This might have reflected the egalitarian ethos: that in Norway we wanted everybody to think for themselves, not just follow a leader.

The 'retreat of the social' that occurred during the late 1990s – and maybe we're still feeling the end of that period – was a difficult time for ethnography.[10] As Thomas [Hylland Eriksen] said this morning, that's when they stole our clothes while we were out swimming. You've all experienced that. And I think, yes, while we retreated from the social (of what we have labelled 'social anthropology') we carried on with our business as usual, we did write ethnography, we did our work. But we need now to again address the social; we need to again step out and think.

And in Oslo we used that evaluation whether we agreed with it or not. I think, yes, I agree with Penny [Harvey], we've always been international, we've always had these relationships; but yes, we can be more actively engaged with the world. Maybe in different ways than in the earlier 'big man' systems, but still – we tried to organize our project in Oslo around three major groups.[11] One studied economy, one studied ritual and one studied domestication practices.

---

10   The 'emptying of significance' from society and social life has been seen as indicative of individualist and subjectivist turns in anthropology, which for critical anthropological observers were deemed inextricably tied to 'larger political processes of neo-liberalism and neo-conservatism' (Kapferer 2005:2–3).

11   The project 'Anthropos and the Material' at the Department of Social Anthropology, University of Oslo, was one of five anthropological 'institution-based strategic projects' (ISP) funded by the Research Council of Norway for the period 2013 to 2016. These projects were follow-ups of the international evaluation process of 2010/11. See Bendixsen and Hviding (this volume) 1 for more details on these projects. The Oslo ISP resulted in an edited collection (Harvey *et al.* 2019).

And then we created a shared arena where we met and challenged each other, trying to bring out disagreements, not just the harmonious, homogeneous, egalitarian ethic that we are so good at but which has its downsides: it is kind of difficult to just stand out and discuss theory. But I think that for the sake of the discipline we really need to do so.

Finally, our weakest point is our strength: the way in which our discipline works, and the way in which we work, takes time. We are now being measured in terms of time spent, especially in the PhD programme and how many years it takes for PhDs to be completed, and this we just have to fight against. Because if what we do does not take time, we might as well be doing something else.

Open discussion

Editors' note: Following Ingjerd Hoëm's contribution to the panel discussion, proceedings paused for a twenty-minute tea and coffee break. After the break, moderator Annelin Eriksen opened the discussion again by asking some members of the panel to elaborate specifically on an aspect of the international evaluation of Norwegian anthropology concerning 'theory building'. This opening of the discussion at large then led to a consideration of anthropology's 'usefulness'.

ANNELIN ERIKSEN: Welcome back from the break. While you all think about your questions, and Christine writes names on her list, I'll start with a question directly to the panel. Or, rather, a sequence of questions.

We have heard repeatedly today about the evaluation of Norwegian anthropology, and we have come to know its – by now famous, or infamous – conclusion: We Norwegian anthropologists are great appliers of theory, but not so great developers of theory. My first question, then, has to be: Is this so? Unni [Wikan] has already said that she's not happy with that conclusion. But what if it is true? What if we *are* less interested in theory than we should be? Why is that so? Is there, perhaps, a kind of 'down to earth' character to Norwegian anthropology, a kind of pragmatism that is reflected in a focus on usefulness, relevance and so forth? Could this in turn be a reflection of a more fundamental feature of Norwegian sociality? Can we, for instance, connect this to Fredrik Barth – Halvard Vike talked about this earlier (see Vike, this volume) – a specific form of Norwegian egalitarianism? Is it connected to 'luck', that we believe high theory is for 'high flyers', too individualistic and for the upper classes as it were? Is this why theory appears to be not so strongly developed in Norwegian anthropology? I will ask Marit [Melhuus] and Unni [Wikan] to respond first.

MARIT MELHUUS: Well, that was quite a challenge, Annelin. I'm not sure if this is so or not, but if we are going to go along with your hypothesis that it may be the case – and if I were to paint with a large paintbrush – I would say it might have to do with Norwegian *nyttetenkning*, which means our pervasive utilitarian, pragmatic attitude to knowledge. In fact, even when the University of Oslo was established (some 200 years ago) the whole idea was to build up knowledge in Norway that could be easily translated into something useful. But then, of course, anthropology was never actually created to be useful! There's a problem there, and what I would throw back in response is a reference exactly to this utilitarian way of thinking. Some years ago there was a debate going around in national media about how useful anthropology should – or could – be! And if you look at research funding programmes these days, many of them are oriented toward 'producing' knowledge that can be translated into something useful for society. What we call the 'pure research' grants are fewer and fewer and harder to get, for anthropologists as for anyone else. Which I think would be a good idea to do something with.

UNNI WIKAN: You know, I don't think there is something wrong at all with anthropology having to be useful. Because, well – it *should* be useful. Why should we refuse to consider this? If anthropology could enlighten the community, the people, so on and so forth, that's absolutely what we should aim for.

Concerning theory: I don't agree at all with the perspective that Norwegian anthropology has not taken the stage in building theory. I could say that there are no other anthropologies elsewhere – in the United States or here in Britain – that excel in 'theory building' significantly more than Norwegian anthropology does. But I mean, what is the point of such comparison anyway? What criteria do the evaluation committees use when they say that we are not doing well in theory?

MARION BERGHAHN:[12] As a publisher – and since I think nearly half the people here are my authors – I want to comment from that point of view. Our Norwegian authors and their books have never been found wanting in theory. And furthermore there just cannot be ethnography without any theory. And I can only say: none of our Norwegian authors have ever been criticized by readers, reviewers and so forth in any form for lacking in theory.

MARIT MELHUUS: In his contribution this morning, Gunnar [Sørbø] gave what I think is an excellent example of anthropology generated within an

---

12   Publisher of Berghahn Books.

applied situation, and he showed how it can be used and also how it went back into anthropological theories of knowledge that we can all share. But I would just like to add on a personal note: When I was a student, I was very, very determined that the anthropological knowledge that I was going to produce was going to be useful to people. I have since become a grown up woman! And when I was on the university board and all these new systems were being put in place, I was one – along with other colleagues – who was defending the right of creating knowledge for its own sake. And I will still defend that, the way things are going now. I don't need to see immediate relevance.

Editors' note: At this point, several brief questions and comments about the Norwegian approach to fieldwork were asked from the audience. It was suggested that we needed some discussion of how to define different categories of fieldwork, and there was particular interest among the audience in the concept of fieldwork by students. It was noted by some that in British anthropology departments, fieldwork for the master's degree is generally not an option, in stark contrast, then, with the Norwegian master's degree, for which six months of fieldwork is mandatory, as described by several of the morning's speakers (see previous chapters, this volume). Discussion moderator Christine M. Jacobsen summed up these comments in the following questions to the panel: Maybe we should start unpacking this concept of fieldwork, and consider what we actually mean when we say that fieldwork is at the core of social anthropology. She also suggested that there is some contestation within Norway in terms of how to think about fieldwork.

UNNI WIKAN: About fieldwork? Well, I was saying that I think fieldwork tuition in anthropology in some places in Norway is going downhill. What I see is that many of our students go to places where they spend much of the time just sitting down with people and interviewing them, and then regard the talk that's being talked as being fieldwork. We need to again emphasize [what we believe fieldwork to be]. In all Norwegian universities we have observation and deduction and all that. I fear there is a problem for anthropology when the word 'fieldwork' today actually refers to sitting around and talking, and that's that.

SIDSEL SAUGESTAD: I want to commend Signe [Howell] for keeping the banner flying high for extended, locally based fieldwork. I think it is very important to be reminded of that from time to time, and particularly when we develop academic study programmes. I also want to throw in the concept 'multi-sited' (Marcus 1995). I find 'multi-sited' a very useful concept for fieldwork on certain types of relationships. Let me exemplify this by the development of indigenous organizations. Clearly, they have to be studied locally, because that is where interaction shapes the kinds of marginalization which constitute the basic momentum for the organizations. Then there is the national level, an arena where public anthropology can play a part in trying to change the constrictions imposed on indigenous entitlements and rights. And there is a very important international level, the processes in the United Nations. Jens Dahl has written a very important book about indigenous people in the United Nations (Dahl 2012), describing the indigenous caucus as something very low-key, very individually based, but located sort of right next door to the United Nations building. So, it depends a bit on what we're studying. It's as simple as that, that's all I wanted to say.

TORD AUSTDAL: I believe the question was to reflect on what fieldwork is, and how one does fieldwork. Doing fieldwork for a master's degree is always, I guess, filled with romanticism about actually doing it for the first time. But in Bergen at least, you do not do your very first fieldwork for your master's – you do it in your first term as an undergraduate! All our first-year undergraduate anthropology students have to carry out a 'mini fieldwork' project on a local scene of some kind. And I think from that moment on, fieldwork is engrained in you to some degree. But fieldwork at the master's level is of course different. It is much more comprehensive. As for me, for my master's degree, I did seven months of fieldwork first and then two months later. When thinking about what it is that one does, I think it is very characteristic that we are educated as anthropology students into what I think is an empiricist approach where you always look for social interaction, as well as all kinds of situations including conflict – all of which is of course very much in a British anthropological tradition in many respects. This is also something that I think remains relevant as a fieldwork strategy, also when engaged in multi-sited work. You can still retain this and you do not have to resort to simple interviewing.

SIGNE HOWELL: Thank you. Well, having sort of opened this discussion on fieldwork, in fact I also was initially sceptical about master's students doing fieldwork. When I first came to Norway, I had this notion of nine months minimum, and I was sceptical of this Norwegian practice at the start. But I sort of changed my mind, and one of the reasons I think I did is that before I came to Oslo, I taught at the University of Edinburgh. And there, in those days at any rate, they had a four-year undergraduate course that ended up with a master's degree. For the final two years they concentrated exclusively on anthropology, they were called junior and senior honours students, and during the third year (or junior honours) the students in fact went off to do fieldwork. And David Shankland, who was one of my students at one time, started by going off by himself to Morocco, I remember – for some four months? – and he came back and wrote very interesting things on the basis of that experience. And that is what a lot of those honours students did. They went to Morocco, they went to Melanesia, they went to wherever took their fancy. And in a way that was a crazy system, unique in the UK. But, you know, the students benefited a lot from what they did, and I kind of carried that experience with me to Norway.

We thought a lot when the Bologna reform was introduced and we got a two-year master's degree. We were very concerned about the level, and also about the reduction of the undergraduate degree – from four years as it had been previously to three years. The only difference was that it was meant to be absolutely full-time studies. So our students would, at least in practice, study full-time for three years, instead of being perhaps more on-and-off for four and a half years.

Anyway, the point is that I think that when we wanted the two-year master's degree to include about six months of fieldwork, we discussed it a lot. And it's not perfect. They now only have one term of preparation before they go off, and that's very, very intensive. For me, the key question is what sort of *footing* the students get once they are out in the field. When we look at what they have when they come back and the kind of dissertations they submit, they are not bad! And yes, obviously some of them do sit around in cafés in cities in Latin America and do little else; maybe they weren't considering becoming anthropologists in the first place, I think.

I've been talking a little bit with the master's students about what happens when they return home from their fieldwork. They have one year, or two terms, to take a few courses and to write up. And the atmosphere then is one of incredibly engaged students who read a lot before they start writing their dissertations. And as I said, their theses are by and large really not bad. They are perfectly respectable. And when they make that annual book with articles based on their fieldwork, of course it is all very self-selective. It's very, virtually – well, I was going to say undisciplined; it's okay, it's okay. And so I'm not so worried about it anymore!

PENNY HARVEY: I'm sort of going backwards. I want to say something about theory, just to pick up on the idea of what it means to produce theory, and why there may be problems. Now I can't see that it should be a problem to be specific to Norway. It seems to be that if you are producing theory, you're trying to create kind of a mode of generalization that encapsulates things into a particular form which then becomes generative. The real criticism in that evaluation seems to be that Norwegian anthropology isn't being generative enough of more things. This is kind of surprising (and maybe it's something typically Norwegian) but the criticism came up that you weren't being sufficiently theoretical. That just seems quite a strange way to criticize institutions, for not being generative enough. For if the tradition at hand is more empirical, then you'd expect empirical work to actually generate concepts that aren't necessarily theoretical – in the sense of kind of producing overarching patterns.

In empirical fieldwork, even if you should be just 'sitting around' in a Latin American city, you might actually be looking at which concepts matter to people, how those concepts structure people's engagements, what those concepts do in people's lives – and all of that could be extremely generative for a way of producing theory on the mobility of concepts, and even a kind of bigger comparative project. Let us say that out of a specialization around the actual comes theory that makes our work generative.

MARIT MELHUUS: Just a very short comment to what Penny [Harvey] just said. I think it's important to consider who was on that evaluation panel, who it was that proposed that conclusion about theory. They were all international scholars, from the UK, from Denmark and so forth. So you have to look at what they mean when they say what they say. So it is thrown back, actually, at the evaluators.

Editors' note: The discussion now picks up and the two moderators note how the dialogue seems to be spreading out in several directions – about fieldwork, about theory and more. A substantial list of speakers builds up.

KAJA BERG HJUKSE: It was commented on how brave it is to send us all out on fieldwork, and I just want to comment that the most important thing for the success of the individual master's student is the supervision. Which is, as we have talked about, arranged in a way that makes it very different from individual to individual. If anything, I think that supervision is key for this form of fieldwork and for the master's thesis to be a good one. The second point was that one of the good things about the master's fieldwork we haven't talked about is that we are allowed to create our own networks independent of supervisors, which I think is a strength.

SUSANNE KÜCHLER:[13] I'm from the anthropology department at UCL. I have quite a few colleagues here today, and some students, including second year undergraduates, were here earlier this morning. We have a 'four-field' department – now even a five-field, sort of – and we actually have at least eight master's programmes, including documentary film, digital anthropology

---

13   Susanne Küchler is professor of material culture at University College London and
     between 2010 and 2019 was head of the UCL department of anthropology.

and so forth. This makes for a great degree of specialism, proliferating even more over fifteen years of funding pressures. The result is certainly PhD students that are highly specialized now, specialized in very particular kinds of fieldwork and theory. And so it is a very interesting question how this would be perceived in Norway. That 'generalist' tradition is, I think, still found here in the UK, but most certainly I can see the next generation of anthropologists coming out of UCL being very, very particularist.

But my real question concerns something that was mentioned in the very first talk this morning (see Smedal, this volume), which was about museums and their importance and the closeness of ethnographic museums and anthropology departments in Norway, which seems not to be common here in the UK at all. So I wondered what sort of platform this sort of closeness creates, not just for fieldwork and research as such, but also regarding training and theory in general.

INGJERD HOËM: The museums are venues for a certain 'contract' with the public that we don't have in the same way in the ordinary departments. So in many of our research projects, we have some kind of components that present projects to the public through museums. That's one way of collaborating. The anthropologists who are in the museums, like in the ethnographic section at the museum of cultural history in Oslo or in Bergen – they are trained as anthropologists but they don't do much ordinary teaching, they work as curators in the museums, though they do supervise graduate students in the departments. So we have some close collaboration in that respect. And since the museums don't have their own PhD programmes, the candidates who have PhD fellowships in the museums take their degrees through the departments. So in that respect, too, there's close collaboration. What this implies for research, is that in former times there was a greater tendency at the museums to study 'material culture', in ways not necessarily seen in the departments. Today, we see more convergence. In conclusion: we are following each other in terms of developing anthropology.

TIM JENKINS:[14] Slightly reframing the discussion, I have been struck by listening to how there seems to be a sort of amiable closeness between Norwegian social anthropology and the Norwegian state. One of these scenes has to do with your internal policies, given that anthropologists work with minorities – but you also do your work abroad with foreign policies. Now, in a lot of countries these would be deeply controversial activities. You can imagine, in Britain, dealing with the troubles of minorities on behalf of the state could be a difficult matter. I just wanted to hear some sort of comment

---

14 Tim Jenkins, Reader in Anthropology and Religion, University of Cambridge.

from some of the speakers about whether or not there are multiple views in Norway on how to relate to the state, or whether it is simply a matter of general consensus; and on what conditions we might figure that could change.

INGJERD HOËM: Just a short comment, for I'm sure there will be more. We had a different political climate some years ago where, for example, multiculturalism was okay, and anthropology as a result had many more students than it has now. On the current political scene, multiculturalism is not such a good thing to promote, and anthropology suffers, with fewer students. Thomas Hylland Eriksen, who had to leave London before this discussion started, could have said more about this. He did get bad press in Norway for his support of multiculturalism, and some might not take him 'seriously' as an academic because of that. At least that is how it would seem. So, certainly, there may be difficulties with the multiculturalist position, also with regard to anthropology's 'reputation'.

GUNNAR M. SØRBØ: Of course, there have been different roads in terms of our participation in, or at least our being close to, Norwegian foreign policy. In the case of Sudan, which I particularly mentioned in my talk, our main continuous concern has been to let local voices be heard. Norway has been very active in Sudan, entwined with peace negotiations, and not very successfully. As anthropologists we have remained on the critical side of many of these issues, but not in the sense that we have been totally on the sidelines. We are still being heard, I think, and particularly now it's very critical in South Sudan. As an anthropologist, I cannot believe in the kind of elite bargains that they are trying to push in South Sudan. I still believe that we have to do something at the local level: the scope is much wider than just conflict between elites, and it has come so far that you have accusations of genocide, and you have subcultures of ethnic violence. A lot of things remain to be done on the ground. And right there is a very important role for anthropologists. But also in the processes at diplomatic levels, there are important anthropological voices to be heard. We know that some of our North American colleagues have been quite vocally engaged in South Sudan, Sharon Hutchinson being one example.

And as was said earlier today, in many ways we remain a small-scale society in Norway. If you are a professor of anthropology, you're likely to know the minister of foreign affairs or the state secretary; we have these rather dense networks. And it makes for some kind of influence, although that is also an issue in itself – to what extent do we have 'impact'? It's something that Signe [Howell] has been writing about (see Howell 2010). It's not always the case. But we have to make our voices heard.

Editors' note: As brief questions and comments from the floor continued, the discussion was steered by the moderators in the direction of a summary of foreign policy issues and towards some interest expressed on the particular role of anthropology in the school system of Norway.

SIDSEL SAUGESTAD: I think Norway's foreign policy has two sorts of banners. We – as in the Norwegian state – like to make peace, and have a concern for indigenous peoples, which, it must be said, has been bordering on missionary attitudes at times. And it's been rightly pointed out that Norway has been very concerned about the indigenous peoples of other countries – which is of course much easier than dealing with its own business at home. There are quite clearly political ups and downs in this, and I think there are quite a few countries that have been annoyed at Norwegian interference and how Norway, even now, with the rainforest being a main issue, has supported groups which may, as some perceive it, be protesting against development, referring to indigenous rights. By and large, I would say that Norway has been toning down this engagement considerably, and any new government might behave differently.

INGJERD HOËM: Thanks for that question from the floor about the 'famous' case of anthropology being taught in schools in Norway. Well in fact, the anthropology that is taught in our schools tends to put young people off any thought of subsequently studying anthropology! As far as the relevant curriculums are concerned, I'm really sorry to say that they are so bad that those who suffer through them don't go on to study anthropology, which is a serious concern. We should definitely do something about it. And so, yes: we are very pleased that anthropology is integrated into our school curriculums, but not in the way we see today. Many years ago Arne Martin Klausen lobbied for anthropology to be a school subject, so that people with an anthropology degree could become mainstream teachers.[15] That's the history, but since then it has taken on a life of its own and we're not so happy with it at the moment. But we'll hopefully be able to tell you a better story next time we meet.

MARIT MELHUUS: I just want to add to what Ingjerd [Hoëm] said about school, and I refer back to what was said this morning about Norwegian public engagement. I also have Arne Martin Klausen in mind, because one of his accomplishments for anthropology in the 1950s and 1960s was to make anthropology a 'valid discipline' for teaching geography in secondary schools.

---

15 Arne Martin Klausen (1927–2018) was professor of social anthropology at the University of Oslo from 1973.

You could teach geography with an anthropology degree. This was actually a big way of making anthropology available in school because of the way education was structured in terms of who can teach what. So, anthropologists would teach geography.

MARTIN THOMASSEN: Regarding the fact that in most European schools, except in Norway, there are no curriculums in anthropology – it is not taught to those not enrolled in university. I have just come back from the EASA meeting in Prague, and everybody spoke about the non-existence of anthropology in the school system.[16] So in fact very few young people in Europe know anything about anthropology before they enter the university, and at the EASA meeting colleagues were quite intrigued to learn a little more about how the Norwegian school system works in this regard. I should say, you've already heard a little through previous comments: although we do have anthropology in our schools, it is not really working. For example, teachers seem to think that social anthropology is good because cultural relativism is something that everybody should aspire to as a goal, as opposed to have it as a method through which to investigate and hopefully discover diversity. So there we get off to a wrong start, because most of these young people have a sense of being globally connected, and just talking about radical difference makes no sense to me. We need to improve the school system's usual approach to anthropology.

CHRISTINE M. JACOBSEN: Moving on now from anthropology in Norwegian schools, I want to pick up on some questions of different influences and approaches that are played out in contemporary anthropology in Norway. This morning, perhaps particularly in the first set of presentations, I somehow got the feeling that the history of Norwegian anthropology sort of ended in the 1990s. Are anthropologists in Norway no longer making history? Or is it just that developments after 1990 are still part of the 'present', and thus absent from 'the history of Norwegian anthropology' rather than an actual sign that Norwegian anthropology no longer makes significant contributions? Alternatively, is it the case of who is telling the history of Norwegian anthropology, and how the narrators are positioned in relation to different anthropological times? Does anyone in the panel wish to speak to that?

---

16   At its annual general meeting in Prague 2015, the European Association of Social Anthropologists organized a two-day seminar entitled 'Making Anthropology Matter'.

OLAF H. SMEDAL: Well, I think that in terms of the history of Norwegian anthropology, the last fifteen to twenty years are actually contemporary! It's more a question of looking at present diversity, which for two reasons has become much greater than it used to be. For ethnographic and financial reasons, small departments became big. The number of students has grown enormously, and if we look at student numbers in the mid 1990s, that really says something about the many young people who wanted to study anthropology, at least for a couple of years. Then at the same time, a flood of government funding for higher education made it possible to hire more permanent staff members, as well as extra assistants for additional seminars to deal with all these new students, a proportion of whom we were in due course able to send on master's degree fieldwork all over the globe. This is what we see reflected here today, and it is the kind of diversity that Synnøve [Bendixsen] spoke about in her talk (Bendixsen, this volume). So it was actually a history up to the late 1980s that I was responsible for, and then Synnøve took over, perhaps. So, it's not over yet. But that story will be summed up in another thirty years!

ANNELIN ERIKSEN: Another question – if there aren't others on the list – is on gender, because Norway profiles itself internationally as the leading nation in terms of gender equality. So, the question for the panel to think about, is whether this has in any way paved the way on the one hand for female anthropologists working in the different departments, and on the other hand for feminist perspectives in anthropology. Has this tendency in Norwegian self-identity – to be very concerned about gender equality – helped gender perspectives, made anthropology more attuned to gender perspectives and paved the way for female anthropologists? Maybe Marit [Melhuus] wants to start?

MARIT MELHUUS: I don't think I can answer this. But I can come up with an example which I already mentioned to Gunnar [Sørbø] earlier today, and I would like to use this opportunity also to say that there are two questions from this afternoon that are still going around in my mind. Now, in the 1970s there was actually quite a strong gender movement among students of anthropology, and elsewhere in the universities. And a group of us actually went actively to work towards Norad, Norway's development agency, in order to incorporate – well, at that time it was women and not gender – to incorporate 'women and development'. And we were actually a group that lobbied quite strongly, and succeeded to a point. Which speaks of what it is possible to achieve politically.

Otherwise, I think gender in anthropology has become kind of a sad story – on two fronts, actually. We had a very strong teaching programme and syllabus focused on gender at the time when Signe [Howell] arrived. Do you remember, Signe? We had a course on gender and religion and those kinds of things? Then all of a sudden – maybe not all of a sudden, actually – gender seemed to dissipate. It was as if there was an attitude of 'all right, we've done it, everybody knows now that they should include gender', and somehow, gender was no longer included. You can see that in many things going on now in our anthropology, with the gender dimension no longer being strong. I think I was commenting to someone here that we need to raise that banner again. And then when it comes to staff – well, I mean, in the department in Oslo we were fifty-fifty women and men for quite a long time. And now, what are we, Ingjerd? Twenty-eighty? Maybe something like 20 per cent women and 80 per cent men. Something has happened in our hiring policies – maybe unwittingly, unconsciously, I hope. This has developed and we haven't been aware of what's happening – and all of a sudden we've come down to twenty-eighty. That's the empirical situation.[17] Why, and what to do about it, that is another question. An important thing to add, and I don't know if that's the situation in Britain too, is that our student body's still overwhelmingly female.

CHRISTINE M. JACOBSEN: Although I am only one of the moderators of this discussion, I have to speak now as the director of the Centre for Women's and Gender Research in Bergen! I think there are maybe two separate things here. I do agree that gender has largely disappeared – off the radar, so to speak – and that we need to look not only at why that is so, but also at how things have been transformed. Part of what has happened is that questions that were crucial to feminist anthropology and gender studies more broadly have been rearticulated, and are now being discussed under different headings such as intersectionality, postcolonialism, queer perspectives. But I also think that the kind of theorizing of gender and feminism that I experienced as a student in Bergen is no longer present in such an explicit sense, which I think is sad.

ANNELIN ERIKSEN: I think Edvard [Hviding] has signalled that the end of this part of today's proceedings is drawing near. I think this has been a wonderful discussion. I want to thank the panel and the audience for bringing up such a range of very important dimensions of Norwegian anthropology and anthropology in Britain and in general: questions to do with theory, fieldwork, museums, foreign policy, education, gender and much more. Thank you very much!

---

17 *Editors' note*: A quick overview of the four anthropology departments in Norway in 2019 gives a total of forty-seven permanent staff members, eighteen of whom are women. The proportions of women to men are (again, indicatively): Oslo 5/11; Bergen 8/7; Trondheim 3/7; Tromsø 2/4.

EDVARD HVIDING: Friends and colleagues, anthropologists have been getting into deep discussions here, and we have been keeping ourselves very busy. This has been an extremely interesting day, not least anthropologically speaking! We now have to move to the next stage of our Norwegian Anthropology Day. I know that that our friends at the RAI will soon have drinks available for us just outside. But before that, I have a very special occasion that I wish to announce. As you all know, every form of symposium has to reach its proper end, but such events can end in many different ways. I have been to meetings and conferences – even symposiums – that turned heavy and intellectually congested at the end of the day and sort of just floated out and away. But this particular event is not going to end like that, for we have a rare privilege today. Our frequent 'Norway friend' – a good vernacular concept that has been introduced – our 'Norway friend' Professor Marilyn Strathern has very graciously agreed to come down from Cambridge to be with us today and to close off the event with her remarks. Marilyn, it is such a privilege to have you here. We know that you're busy, and in such demand, by so many different parties. We didn't take it for granted that you would be coming. Indeed, we had an original date planned that we had to shift, so you have actually been very accommodating and more than generous. We appreciate that deeply. Colleagues, friends, may I introduce to you: Dame Marilyn Strathern.

References

Dahl, J. 2012. *The Indigenous Space and Marginalized Peoples in the United Nations*. New York: Palgrave MacMillan.

Harvey, P., Krohn-Hansen, C. and Nustad, K. (eds). 2019. *Anthropos and the Material*. Durham, NC: Duke University Press.

Hastrup, K., Garsten, C., Hansen, T.B., Mitchell, J.P. and Vuorela, U.M. 2011. 'Social and cultural anthropological research in Norway: an evaluation'. Oslo: Research Council of Norway, Division of Science.

Howell, S. 2010. 'Norwegian academic anthropologists in public spaces'. *Current Anthropology* 51: S269–S277.

Kapferer, B. 2005. 'Introduction: the social construction of reductionist thought and practice'. In B. Kapferer, (ed.), *The Retreat of the Social: The Rise and Rise of Reductionism*, pp. 1–18. Oxford: Berghahn Books.

Marcus, G. 1995. 'Ethnography in/of the world system: the emergence of multi-sited ethnography'. *Annual Review of Anthropology* 24:95–117.

9

Norwegian anthropology

Towards the identification of an object

Marilyn Strathern

✦

Editors' note: Professor Strathern's perceptive closing remarks were in large measure improvised by her as a reflection on the course of the day's proceedings, as will be seen from her frequent references to speakers. It was the intention of neither her nor the organizers that she would submit a written text for publication. However, Dame Marilyn's talk proved so inspirational, and the sound recording so clear, that we organized a provisional transcription. Only slight editorial changes have been made, and the following remarks are included in the book with our deep appreciation both of her uncanny ability to draw together the day's multiple and disparate strands into a memorable set of observations, and of her own long-standing friendly and supportive relationships with her Norwegian colleagues. We thank Professor Strathern for agreeing to have her closing comments published.

This has been a terrific and quite remarkable occasion. We have had a series of presentations this morning, a very lively panel discussion and an even livelier and extremely well-orchestrated discussion to follow. There have been, as one might imagine, diverse perspectives, points of view and analyses.

I have nothing new to say at all, nor am I going to gloss what has been said. But I do want to put one or two thoughts in your heads. Let me first of all begin on a personal note. I was delighted to be asked to be part of today's proceedings, and to become more fully aware of things that I only half knew. As so often in anthropology, interest in specific pursuits is bound up with the respect one has for colleagues involved in them. And I have known and admired many such colleagues from Norway – and I could not, of course, resist the invitation! But the rubric of the day sort of struck me as odd. Of course, we are familiar with different traditions in anthropology, different institutional and bureaucratic frameworks, different schools of thought, the roles of international relations and so forth. And Norway, and Scandinavia at large, certainly has a unique place in Europe's anthropology. Yet the immediacy of the country name – somehow in my head it was 'Norway Day' (I do realize it's in fact Norwegian Anthropology Day) – brought me up short or, rather, made me very curious.

When one gathers together scholars from a particular country, what does that rubric of such a gathering do, in terms of them seeing themselves and their discipline? In your shoes, how would I present myself as a UK, or a British or a Welsh anthropologist? What would I pick on to tether me to that category? Would it be practices of teaching, significant past figures that influenced what people taught and learnt; or self-conscious intellectual positions, born of cultivated discursive media; or encouragement or lack of encouragement from the state; or identified genealogies and pathways of interest, ethnographic starting points or cross- disciplinary collaborations?

I would hesitate to find distinctiveness in one or other of these dimensions, although at the general level we did have some reference to a 'collective spirit' today. But I'd be very interested to find distinctiveness in conventions of language use and vernacular and technical conceptualizations – or perhaps some insights into what others might find puzzling or even incomprehensible – or conditions of possibility – all of these. So I came here today very curious to find out what 'Norway' or 'Norwegian' might mean. Would it emerge as an epistemological object, perhaps? Or rather, what kind of object was going to emerge, if any?

Before I turn to a comment or two on that, let me just say what immediately came to my mind with the thought of 'Norway'. One word: *hospitality*. In both Bergen and Oslo I have been the happy recipient of unsurpassed hospitality, in equal amounts of good cheer and intellectual stimulus. And whatever stirred people to dream up visiting scholar programmes or international collaboration, there is a generosity – and I include intellectual generosity – to the way in which colleagues in Norway share themselves and their work with others. And if you will allow me a personal recollection in which that merit is indirectly referred to: twenty-seven years ago, and really in a very formative sense for me, there was a gathering of gender scholars from all over Norway – an event which was itself held in Bergen – and that gathering has marked Norway in my mind.

When thinking of how to answer my own question about what kind of object was going to emerge, I thought: 'Oh, there's one obvious object that's going to emerge'. And, my father had a phrase, 'bet your bottom boots'.

And so I bet my bottom boots that at some point Norwegian anthropology had to emerge as a *bureaucratic* object. There would be a situation, within institutional media, the governmental state, the university, or whatever, when that was surely going to have to surface at some point. I had no idea it would surface the moment that Edvard [Hviding] rose to his feet. In his very first – I'm not sure if it was in his first sentence – but in his very first remarks, he delineated the bureaucratic object. Because he told us that the whole *idea* for a day on Norwegian anthropology had been stimulated by the national assessment exercise. And Norwegian anthropology was thereby declared, literally, a unit of assessment – and on that basis offered to the RAI, which of course already had a program of 'days of national anthropologies'. And I think we've heard from comments that the Director of the RAI made from the floor about the interest behind getting people together from different countries.

Okay, so we have the bureaucratic object. So that seems to be interesting – and now we know what it is! The first speaker was Olaf [Smedal], if you recall. And he was talking about the role that museums had to play very early on in Norwegian anthropology. And very quickly he gave his object – Norwegian anthropology – another contour. It is an entity that can claim a first! And what can claim a first in this case was the first ethnographic world survey, if you will recall. This entity that can claim a first was subsequently also seen to act – and this is reinforcement – so that the one observation becomes reinforced by the other: Gunnar [Sørbø] claimed another first for Norwegian anthropology. And that was when the first non-economist appointment had been made at a very high-profile level. Right, so we have this bureaucratic object taking shape, and it's one that has a capacity to transmit to future generations achievements of the past, in the form of having claimed a first on the international stage. But that also points to something very interesting about this particular object, and that is that it allows itself to be internally differentiated.

So our object starts acquiring a kind of structure. And we have heard references to a number of theoretical differences between Norwegian universities, between particular individuals and so forth, and that point was repeated again in Synnøve [Bendixsen]'s contribution when she pointed to the importance of there being discussions and debates today, and the significance of the enlarged repertoire of work to this internal diversity. And what that means, of course, is that if you recognize diversity, if you recognize difference, you are recognizing not necessarily a standard from which others are deviating – but you are recognizing that there are core issues about which difference itself becomes significant, so that the very notion of diversity speaks to the fact that individuals and departments are debating over themes that they find it important to debate. So our object is acquiring a certain amount of colour. Signe [Howell] made a very interesting comment in relation to, actually, somebody whose work was quite influential on myself – Marianne Gullestad – in which she suggested that Marianne had actually been on the periphery of Norwegian anthropology.

Okay, so our object is something that can have a periphery to it. And if it has a periphery to it, then what is the periphery surrounding? Well, Signe told us that as well. She very interestingly pointed to the opportunities in the way fieldwork and so forth is structured, which gives various opportunities to those in the system. So being on the periphery, presumably, one isn't allowed to, one isn't in the position of, enjoying opportunities that are there, the resources so to speak, that are at the centre. This of course was a fascinating discussion about different institutional structures.

We came then to Halvard [Vike]'s contribution, and he raised another issue altogether. Not one of what is the periphery and then what might be a centre, or what is diversity and then what might be worth arguing about, but the question of whom one's audience is. And I say that because towards the end of this contribution, he made some very interesting observations about anthropologists' access to the ear of institutions, in the sense of the receptivity of institutions to what anthropology is talking about. He also of course made the comment about anthropologists faced with not just with one community, but with myriads of conflicting audiences. So our object begins to take on a sort of prism-like effect, in which we both have this internal diversity and also a conception of an externally diverse range of audiences to which it is speaking. And the question of audience was raised again when Thomas [Hylland Eriksen] spoke in terms of access to the ear of the media.

Something Gunnar referred to struck a chord. If I understand him correctly, he was talking at one point of various interventions. He said that those interventions came with a programme of hopeful development and improvement of conditions and circumstances, and so forth. It was nothing to do with any particular institutional interest that Norway as a country itself had in that particular country. The chord it struck, although resounding differently, is in the Pacific work that has come out of Bergen, in which Edvard has been involved, ECOPAS, where one of the claims that the university made for its suitability in driving forward this study, was that it was intellectually independent from the nation's interest in the area, as Norway had no previous aid programmes or other stakes in the Pacific. This seems to actually raise a point against the discussion you had about theoretical issues, as though there were some kind of opposition between theorizing and applied work. It struck me that one of the questions one ought to be asking is not whether work is applied or not, but what the interests are of those people who are carrying it out. It seems to me that the crucial divide is between interest and disinterest, not between sort-of-applied and theoretical.

Thomas opened his comments with another delineation of this object, Norwegian anthropology, namely as an object that in itself is capable of self-reflection. You'll recall that he opened by saying that there's always something new to be learnt. And he said one usually learns about oneself, but I think that one could read that also to mean whoever is the author in question, and the author in question here is Norwegian anthropology!

I think I've now lost track of the various images that are eternally differentiating a prismatic object that has various capacities, and also has a capacity for self-reflection. And of course that is what was said in the very last talk, by Synnøve. And what do we discover? After all, Norwegian anthropology is an ethnographic object, and we might, I suppose, have known that all along. But I thought that to be a beautiful end to the morning. And I don't see any need to add to that, but it gave the final shape to whatever it is that I've been describing.

I'm not going to comment on the panel discussions as such, except that obviously the point is that Norwegian anthropology is debatable and an object of debate. That came through. Not because it was simply set up that way – I mean, debates can fail – it takes more than there being a debate in order to say, yes, it's also a debatable object.

I have a final comment. If I commented on what this morning's presentations were like, and derived a rather banal, external characterization from what was in fact a very interesting panel and discussion following, perhaps I could also comment on today as a whole. Something struck me as remarkable about it, and I'm not quite sure if I'm going to find the right words. I may offend people and I don't mean to, or perhaps I do mean to offend people. I certainly can't admit to that, anyway. It's been very good natured, it's been humorous, nobody's dominated the floor, nobody's been taking themselves too seriously, I've not heard people being defensive, I've not heard people being promotional. It's as though anthropologists from Norway, if I can put it that way, don't have to make a point. As though they're comfortable within their skins. I'm not going to say that they didn't generate any conflict, because that would be presumptuous on the non-Norwegian side. But there's a certain self-assurance that was not self-promotional. I suppose one wouldn't really expect it to be otherwise, with what one knows from the writings and so forth. But Thomas actually gave it a little extra definition – I mean he just described it, and what he said was that anthropologists from Norway aren't worried about lightness. And I thought that absolutely summed up the tenor of today.

I began with personal thanks. Let me now end with collective thanks from us all to the organizers, if I may, and also to the RAI.

Contributors

Synnøve K.N. Bendixsen, Associate professor of social anthropology, University of Bergen

Thomas Hylland Eriksen, Professor of social anthropology, University of Oslo

Signe Howell, Professor (emerita) of social anthropology, University of Oslo

Edvard Hviding, Professor of social anthropology, University of Bergen

Olaf H. Smedal, Professor of social anthropology, University of Bergen

Marilyn Strathern, Professor (emerita) of social anthropology, University of Cambridge

Gunnar M. Sørbø, Senior researcher (emeritus), Chr. Michelsen Institute, Bergen

Halvard Vike, Professor of health and welfare studies, University of South-Eastern Norway, and research professor at Telemark Research Institute (Telemarksforsking)

Panellists and moderators

Tord Austdal, Associate professor of social sciences, Faculty of Arts and Education, University of Stavanger

Annelin Eriksen, Professor of social anthropology and vice-rector for global relations, University of Bergen

Penny Harvey, Professor of social anthropology, University of Manchester

Kaja Berg Hjukse, PhD candidate in social anthropology, University of Oslo

Ingjerd Hoëm, Professor of social anthropology, University of Oslo

Christine M. Jacobsen, Professor of social anthropology, University of Bergen

Jan Peter Laurens Loovers, Project curator, British Museum, London

Marit Melhuus, Professor (emerita) of social anthropology, University of Oslo

Sidsel Saugestad, Professor (emerita) of social anthropology, University of Tromsø

Martin Thomassen, Associate professor of social anthropology, Norwegian University of Science and Technology (NTNU)

Unni Wikan, Professor (emerita) of social anthropology, University of Oslo

Index

Page numbers in **bold** refer to chapter authorship.

Aberdeen, University of   116, 117
Amundsen, Roald   36
anthropologists, numbers of   87
Archetti, Eduardo   28, 38, 79, 80, 81
Ask, Karin   64
Aspen, Harald   24
Austdal, Tord   113, 122, 137
Australian Aborigines   21–2, 35–6

Barnes, John   5, 47, 48, 51–2, 54
Barth, Fredrik   4, 44, 49, 55–6, 60, 75, 89,
    90, 116, 117
  critiques of   27, 62
  field research   5, 19, 20, 45, 67
  at Oslo Ethnographic Museum   3, 6,
      7, 12, 19, 27, 35
  published work   5, 20, 23, 28, 29,
      34–5, 37, 49, 50, 62, 108
  at University of Bergen   23, 26, 37,
      61, 62
Bendixsen, Synnøve K.N.   vii, viii, 1, 2, 10,
    26, **86**, 112, 129, 134, 136, 137
Bennike, Pia   18
Bergen, University of, anthropology
    department   3, 14, 23, 37, 62, 87, 105,
    111, 130
  fieldwork   7–8, 38
  Institution-based Strategic
      Projects   vii, 2, 91
  Professor II posts   102, 103, 113
  research projects   2, 88, 89
  visiting lecturers   5, 34
  see also Centre for Development
      Studies; Centre for Women's and
      Gender Research and Khartoum,
      University of
Berghahn, Marion   120
Berreman, Gerald   5
Bleie, Tone   64
Bloch, Maurice   26
Blom, Jan-Petter   26, 46
Boas, Franz   4
Bohannan, Laura   5
Bohannan, Paul   5
Bologna agreement   35, 39–40, 123
Bourdieu, Pierre   29

British anthropology
  differences from Norwegian
      anthropology   103, 116–17
  influence on Norwegian
      anthropology   4, 19–20, 30, 122
British Museum   116
Brøgger, Jan   3, 110
Brox, Ottar   23, 49–50, 51, 62, 63
Brundtland, Gro Harlem   25

Cambridge, University of   20, 125
Centre for Development Studies   64, 89
Centre for Women's and Gender
    Research   101, 130
Chr. Michelsen Institute   2, 64
colonial history, Norwegian   16–17, 55, 103
conferences and symposia   3, 5, 39, 65–6,
    90, 92, 116, 91
CULCOM   38

Dahl, Jens   122
Danielsen, Tone   77
Denmark-Norway   17
development and anthropology   60–9, 135
Døving, Runar   78, 81
Dumont, Louis   6

EASA see European Association of Social
    Anthropologists
Edinburgh, University of   122
egalitarianism   48, 54, 114, 118, 119
  Bergen project   89
  'equality as sameness' concept   6, 46,
      47, 51, 95
Eidheim, Harald   5, 19, 25, 26
Enzensberger, Hans Magnus   54
Epstein, A.L.   5
ERC see European Research Council
Eriksen, Annelin   101, 119, 129, 130, 137
Eriksen, Thomas Hylland   10, 12, 29, 38,
    61, 68, **73**, 89, 95, 108, 110, 118, 126, 135,
    136, 137
Ethnic Groups and Boundaries   5, 62, 108
Ethnographic Museum, Oslo   3, 6–7, 12,
    18–19, 23, 27, 36, 60, 105, 106; see also
    'Loft crowd'

ethnography   3, 4, 6, 13, 20, 21, 22, 23, 56,
   91, 103, 118
   first ethnographic world survey   18,
      134
European Association of Social
   Anthropologists (EASA)   128
European Economic Community
   referendums   26, 27, 50, 51
European Research Council (ERC)   89
evaluation of research, audit-oriented   2,
   90, 104–5, 107, 118, 124
Evans-Pritchard, Edward E.   20, 35
exhibitions   36

Falkenberg, Aslaug   22
Falkenberg, Johannes   4, 20–2, 35
Ferguson, James   28
fieldwork   1, 13–14, 17, 96, 106, 108, 121–3
   'at home', in Norway   7, 28, 37, 38,
      45–9, 115
   duration of   7, 34, 40, 93, 122, 123
   future of   93
   international   21–2, 23, 25–6, 34,
      35–6, 38–9, 114–15
   see also 'home blindness'
Firth, Raymond   5, 35, 38, 69
Fortes, Meyer   35
Foucault, Michel   30
French anthropology   4
   influence on Norwegian
      anthropology   14, 26
Freud, Sigmund   110
Friedman, Jonathan   26
funding for research
   European Research Council   89
   and oil industry   96, 103, 117
   Research Council of Norway   35,
      38–9, 64, 87, 89
   see also Institution-based Strategic
      Projects (ISPs)

Geertz, Clifford   29
Gellner, Ernest   43
gender
   balance in anthropology   107, 129, 130
   research on   101, 129–30
Gjessing, Gutorm   18, 19, 20, 23, 60
Gluckman, Max   5
Godelier, Maurice   26, 38
Goffman, Erving   5, 88, 110
grants *see* funding for research
Grønhaug, Reidar   66, 76

Gullestad, Marianne   5–6, 28, 29, 37, 46,
   47, 51, 52, 78, 95, 135
Gupta, Akhil   28

Haaland, Gunnar   61, 62, 64, 67
Harald V, King of Norway   25
Harvey, David   105
Harvey, Penny   102, 106, 114, 117, 118, 123,
   124, 137
Hastrup, Kirsten   28
Henriksen, Georg   63
Heyerdahl, Thor   36
higher education in Norway
   degree structures   35
   reform under Bologna Process   35,
      39–40, 88, 90, 123
history of anthropology in Norway   2–7,
   16–30, 128–9
Hjukse, Kaja Berg   114, 124, 137
Hoëm, Ingjerd   117, 125, 126, 127, 137
'home blindness'   8, 42–4, 50, 93
Howell, Signe   7, 26, **34**, 121, 122, 126,
   129–30, 134, 137
Hutchinson, Sharon   126
Hviding, Edvard   vii, viii, **1**, 89, 101, 117,
   130, 131, 134, 137

indigenous peoples   25, 36–7, 109, 121–2,
   127; *see also* Australian Aborigines *and*
   Sámi
Ingold, Tim   27
Ingstad, Helge   36
Institute of Comparative Cultural
   Research   38
Institute for Social Research   6
Institution-based Strategic Projects
   (ISPs)   vii, 2, 91–2, 118
institutionalization of anthropology in
   Norway   3–5, 22–4
international engagement   102–3, 104, 118
   fieldwork   21–2, 23, 25–6, 34, 35–6,
      38–9, 114–15
   publishing   90, 91–2
International Work Group for Indigenous
   Affairs   25
ISPs *see* Institution-based Strategic Projects

Jacobsen, Christine M.   101, 102, 121, 128,
   130, 137
James, Wendy   34, 38
Jenkins, Tim   125
journals   3, 92, 94

Kapferer, Bruce 89, 92
Khartoum, University of 9, 38, 61, 64, 109
Klausen, Arne Martin 4, 12, 26, 28, 35, 36,
 60, 95, 127
Kleivan, Helge 25, 26
knowledge
 pragmatic attitude to 119–21
 and technology 110–11
Kraft, Jens 6, 18
Kramer, Julian 28
Küchler, Susanne 124
Kundera, Milan 73, 74, 78, 80, 82

Ladstein, Miriam viii
Larsen, Tord 26, 95
Leach, Edmund 5, 19, 20
Leem, Kurt 4
Lévi-Strauss, Claude 21
Lid, Nils 18, 20
'Loft crowd' 3, 6–7, 19–22, 23, 25–6, 35
London School of Economics 19
London, University College 124
Loovers, Jan Peter Laurens 116, 137
Lumholtz, Carl 4, 6, 17, 35–6

Malinowski, Bronisław 4, 17, 20, 35, 93
Manchester, University of, anthropology
 department 5, 25, 92
Marxist influence on Norwegian
 anthropology 7, 26, 29, 38, 106
master's degree 114–16, 121, 123, 124
Mauss, Marcel 110
Mayer, Adrian 5
McLuhan, Marshall 83
Meillassoux, Claude 26
Melhuus, Marit 64, 111, 120, 124, 127, 129,
 137
Mette-Marit, Crown Princess of
 Norway 87
Mitchell, J. Clyde 5, 76
museums, ethnographic
 role in Norwegian anthropology 16,
 17, 125
 see also Ethnographic Museum, Oslo

Nansen, Fridtjof 36
Needham, Rodney 21–2
New Public Management 54, 75, 81, 86
Nielsen, Yngvar 18
Nietzsche, Friedrich 73
Norad see Norwegian Agency for
 Development Cooperation

Norsk Antropologisk Forening 3, 39, 90,
 92, 94
Norsk Antropologisk Tidsskrift 3, 92, 94
Norwegian Agency for Development
 Cooperation (Norad) 61, 63, 68, 129
Norwegian Anthropological Association
 see Norsk Antropologisk Forening
Norwegian anthropology 1–2, 86–97, 106
 distinctiveness 133–6
 generalism 111–13
 history 2–7, 16–30, 128–9
 and periphery 92–3, 105, 109, 135
 trajectory 7–11
Norwegian Anthropology Day (London; 30
 October 2015) vii–viii, 1, 2, 91
 chapter contributions 6–11, 16–99
 closing remarks 11, 132–6
 panel discussion 11, 100–31
Norwegian cultural and social
 attitudes 28, 46–9, 53–4, 95
Norwegian Ethnological Society 20
Norwegian University of Science and
 Technology 110
Norwegians
 misinterpretation of
 anthropologists 10, 80–2
 relationship with state 53–4, 125–6
 see also public anthropology

Ødegaard, Cecilie 103
oil industry and funding for
 anthropology 28, 103, 117
Oslo Ethnographic Museum see
 Ethnographic Museum, Oslo
Oslo, University of, anthropology
 department 3, 7–8, 23, 35, 37, 38–9,
 105, 107, 111, 130
 fieldwork 7, 38–40
 Institution-based Strategic
 Projects 91, 118
 PhD programme 39–40, 114
 research projects 2, 88
 students 4, 40, 45

Paine, Robert 25, 27
panel discussion 11, 100–31
PhD students
 diversity of research 114
 employment 103, 114
 evaluation 119
 supervision 113
political anthropology in Norway 49–55,
 75

Popper, Karl 63
pragmatic attitudes to knowledge 119–21
public anthropology 10, 49, 73–83, 96,
110, 127–8
publishing 120
international publications 90, 91–2
language policies 57, 94, 103

Radcliffe-Brown, Alfred 4, 17, 19, 21, 22,
35
Research Council of Norway (RCN)
funding of research 35, 38–9, 64,
87, 89
Institution-based Strategic Projects
(ISPs) vii, 2, 91–2, 118
Royal Anthropological Institute (RAI)
and national anthropologies 134
RAI Country Series 1
see also Norwegian Anthropology Day
Rudie, Ingrid 26, 38

Sahlins, Marshall 76
Sámi 3, 4, 5, 21, 24–6, 35, 38, 108–9, 116
Saugestad, Sidsel 108, 116, 121, 127, 137
Schober, Elisabeth 89
school curriculum, anthropology in 127–8
Shankland, David vii, 122–3
Siverts, Henning 23, 26, 37
Smedal, Olaf H. 6, **16**, 35, 37, 109, 129,
134, 137
Solberg, Ole Martin 18, 20, 21
Solheim, Jorun 62
Sommerfelt, Axel 19, 20, 25, 35
Sørbø, Gunnar M. 9, **60**, 89, 109, 120, 126,
134, 135, 137
Sørhaug, Hans Christian 46–7, 79, 81,
82, 95
Sørum, Arve 36
state, Norwegian relationship with 53–4,
125–6
Stavanger, University of 113

Stenius, Henrik 53
Stølen, Kristi Anne 64
Strathern, Marilyn vii–viii, 11, 28, 29, 44,
131, **132**, 137
Sudan, anthropological collaboration in 9,
38, 61, 64–7, 126–7
Sundt, Eilert 4, 45
supervision, student 113, 124

Talle, Aud 78
Tavistock Institute 23
technology and knowledge 110–11
Terray, Emmanuel 26
theory-building 90, 91, 92, 107–8, 119,
120, 123–4
Thomassen, Martin 109, 128, 137
Tromsø, University of, anthropology
department 3, 6, 23, 24–6, 130
Sámi studies 3, 4, 5, 24–6, 108–9, 116
Trondheim, University of, anthropology
department 3, 24, 109–11, 130
Institution-based Strategic
Projects 91

The Unbearable Lightness of Being 73–4,
78, 80, 82
undergraduate degree 123

Vayda, Andrew 66
Vike, Halvard 8, **42**, 95, 119, 135, 137
Vinson, Amanda vii

Wadel, Cato 28
Wenner-Gren Foundation 5
Burg Wartenstein symposia 65
Wikan, Unni 78, 105, 109, 113, 119, 120,
121, 137
word clouds 94–5
Worsley, Peter 5

www.ingramcontent.com/pod-product-compliance
Lightning Source LLC
Chambersburg PA
CBHW052011270326
41929CB00015B/2877